BRITISH PORCELAIN

BRITISH PORCELAIN

An Illustrated Guide

Geoffrey A. Godden

BARRIE & JENKINS

LONDON

Barrie & Jenkins Ltd
20 Vauxhall Bridge Road, London SW1V 2SA

Copyright © 1974 Geoffrey A. Godden

First published in 1974
Reprinted 1977, 1980, 1986, 1990

ISBN 0 2146 6851 7

Printed by Printer Portuguesa, Portugal

Contents

Contents

Preface

This new book has two reliable and popular parents: firstly, *An Illustrated Encyclopaedia of British Pottery and Porcelain*, with its wealth of illustrations; and secondly, the series of *Illustrated Guides*,[1] dealing in depth with the products of individual factories or with groups of wares, such as Salt-glazed or Parian.

In general, this present book is based on the large *Illustrated Encyclopaedia* which was published in 1966, but now a full new range of instructive photographs is featured. Since this volume is confined to porcelain (there is a companion volume on pottery) an even greater coverage can be made, and the pictorial story has been extended forward from 1900.

This illustrated guide to British porcelain will be found to complement, not to duplicate, the previous *Illustrated Encyclopaedia*, which is still in print and readily available.

The illustrations have been chosen especially to help the reader—the novice as well as the advanced collector—to correctly attribute British porcelains to their real source and period. In particular, the many photographs of the frequently un-marked porcelains of the 1800–1840 period will be found to be helpful, for these wares are seldom illustrated and the porcelains are very often incorrectly attributed. Here the key shapes are recorded, with supporting facts, such as the range of pattern-numbers to be expected on such shapes.

As no general book can hope to compete with specialist reference-books in its coverage of some fashionable and well-documented factories, special regard has been paid here to showing the products of the lesser-known factories, those which as yet have no literature of their own. In the other cases—the Bow and Chelsea factories, for example—a good, typical range of illustrations is given and the reader is referred to the appropriate specialist books for a fuller coverage. Most of the modern books are still in print and available for purchase, but all books cited should be available at public reference libraries or can be obtained, on request, through the excellent inter-library loan scheme. The large library at the Victoria and Albert Museum is recommended for the rarer reference-books, since it is rather more accessible than the better-known British Museum Library, where a reader's ticket is required.

To enable a large and instructive range of illustrations to be included with

---

[1] Titles in this series are *The Illustrated Guide to Lowestoft Porcelain* (G. A. Godden); *The Illustrated Guide to Worcester Porcelain 1751–1793* (H. Sandon); *The Illustrated Guide to Rockingham Pottery and Porcelain* (D. Rice); *The Illustrated Guide to Mason's Patent Ironstone China* (G. A. Godden); *The Illustrated Guide to Liverpool Herculaneum Pottery* (A. Smith); *The Illustrated Guide to Staffordshire Salt-Glazed Stoneware* (A. R. Mountford); *The Illustrated Guide to Victorian Parian China* (C. and D. Shinn). These are now out of print but available in most Public Libraries.

detailed captions, the text has been condensed to the essential outline, and while a very large number of British porcelains are here featured, it is not pretended that every factory or decorating establishment is covered. For example, key pieces from the Brampton and Mansfield Works are shown in *An Illustrated Encyclopaedia of British Pottery and Porcelain*, but as no further marked or inscribed pieces have been reported, I have not included these factories. Also many small Staffordshire firms produced the standard types of bone china in the nineteenth century, and no attempt has been made to show isolated examples from these, often very short-lived, factories. For fuller coverage and for a listing of more than the thousand British porcelain manufacturers, the reader is referred to Geoffrey Godden's *Encyclopaedia of British Porcelain Manufacturers* (Barrie & Jenkins, London, 1988). Similarly, our present knowledge of some little-known eighteenth-century porcelain factories does not permit a pictorial presentation of their products in the present book. Nevertheless, the reader will find a good range of helpful illustrations covering the major British porcelain manufacturers from the 1740s to the present century.

Acknowledgements

For my ability to present this large selection of interesting and, I trust, instructive photographs, I am deeply indebted to many auctioneers and dealers, to several museum curators, to present-day manufacturers, and to numerous private collectors. The sources of the individual illustrations are listed below in alphabetical order.

While I am most grateful for all the kind co-operation that I have received, I sincerely hope that the permanent help that this book may afford to all collectors or students will enable the following persons or concerns to feel that they have contributed to a worthwhile project.

Messrs Bearnes & Waycotts, Torquay, 118.

Mrs L. Black, 321, 323.

I. M. Booth Esq., 441.

Bristol City Art Gallery, 71, 73.

Messrs Bruton, Knowles & Co., 392.

H. E. Chandler Esq., 530.

Chichester Antiques Ltd, 159, 365.

Messrs Christie, Manson & Woods Ltd, 42, 123, 126, 132, 139, 142, 144–45, 153, 167, 172, 178, 189, 231, 234, 246, 254, 259, 261, 267, 271, 332–33, 376, 382, 400, 434, 476, 499, 500, 503, 507.

Messrs Coalport, 461.

The Connoisseur magazine, 279.

Major G. N. Dawnay, 439, 515.

Dudley Delevingue Esq., 314.

Messrs Delomosne & Son Ltd, 131, 152, 180, 473, 485, 487, 490, 495, 543.

Mrs Elizabeth Donaldson, 483.

W. A. Eagle Esq., 292–93.

Mrs Eagleston, 470.

R. J. Evans Esq., 27, 29–30.

Arthur W. Franks Esq., 318.

Messrs Godden of Worthing Ltd, A–B, D–F, 4, 6, 7, 10, 15–16, 24–26, 33, 36, 46, 48–49, 52–54, Colour Plate I, 80–83, 89, 91–93, 95, 98–99, 104,

109, 112, 119, 124, Colour Plate III, 135, 137, 146–48, 150, 158, 161, 165–66, 168, 170, 174–76, 179, 187, 198–99, 203, 207, 210, 212–14, 217–20, 223, 233, 236, 241–42, 244, 248–49, 252, 255–56, 258, Colour Plate V, 260, 262–63, 281, 284, 286–87, 296, 301, 305–6, 312, 316, 320, 339, 348–49, Colour Plate VI, 360, 364, 369–71, 374, Colour Plate VII, 383–84, 387–89, 391, 395, 398–99, 403–4, 408–10, 414–17, 419–25, 433, 435, 440, 442–43, 446, 449, 454–57, 460, 462–64, 469, 471, 477, 479, 482, 484, 489, 494, 496, 510–11, 513, Colour Plate X, 516–17, 523, 527–29, 533, Colour Plate XII, 537, 539, 547, 549–50, 556, 559–62, 564–65.

Dr A. Godfrey, 188

R. E. Graham Esq., 282.

Messrs Graham & Oxley (Antiques), 51.

Messrs Graves, Son & Pilcher, 43, 60, 62.

N. Hare Esq., 138.

Great Yarmouth Museums, 346.

Holburne of Menstie Museum of Art, Bath, 40–41, 240, 330, 478.

J. Hutton Esq., 38.

Ipswich Museums and Art Galleries, 325, 350.

Mr and Mrs F. Langford, 347, 354–56.

J. Lewis Esq., 215, 222, 224.

City of Liverpool Museums, 308–9, 311, 315, 326–27, 520.

Messr Lories, 459.

Messrs Marshall Field & Co., Chicago, 538.

A. Mason Esq., 13–14.

Masons Ironstone China Ltd, 366.

Messrs Mintons Ltd, 396.

Mr and Mrs S. Mitchell, 197, 201, 202, 205.

Mr and Mrs M. Morris, 3, 5, 8, 11–12.

Messrs David B. Newbon, 113, 375.

Mrs O'Donnell, Colour Plate XI.

Parke-Bernet Galleries Inc., 186.

Miss S. Peters, 481, 488, 493.

Messrs Phillips, Auctioneers, 9, 31, 367, 506, 521, 566.

Plymouth City Art Gallery, 72.

R. W. Pococks Esq., 149, Colour Plate IV.

G. S. Proctor Esq., 411.

Messrs Puttick & Simpson (Messrs Phillips Auctioneers), 9, 31, 367, 506, 521, 566.

Mr and Mrs L. E. Reynolds, 50, 56.

Dr D. Rice, 111.

F. E. Ridgway Esq., 453, 358.

Paul B. Riley Esq., 164.

Rotherham Museum, 468, 474.

Royal Crown Derby Co. Ltd (Museum collection), 226, 230, 238, 245.

Messrs Scott, Greenwood & Son Ltd (former publishers of the trade magazine *Pottery Gazette*), 22–23, 275, 426, 557.

Mr and Mrs H. Silwood, 268–70, 280.

Messrs Sotheby & Co., C, 28, 35, 37, 44–45, 47, 57–59, 61, 63–67, 74–75, 79, 101, 105–7, 114–16, 121–22, 127–30, 134, 136, 140–41, 143, 192, 227, 229, 232, 239, 243, 250–51, 253, 264–65, 290–91, 297–98, 310, 317, 324, 335–36, 338, 340, 344, 351, 358, 363, 372, 385, 394, 401–2, 428, 436, 448, 467, 475, 492, 497–98, 501–2, 504, 540–42, 544–45, 548.

Messrs Sotheby's, Belgravia, 427, 429–30, 512, 563.

F. W. Spencer Esq., 466.

Messrs Henry Spencer & Son, 208.

Messrs Spode Ltd, 196, 200, 204, 206, 486, 491.

City Museum and Art Gallery, Stoke-on-Trent, 154, 307, 329.

R. W. Strachan Esq., 100.

Mr and Mrs F. Sutton, 182, 184.

M. Thompson Esq., 195.

Capt. J. W. Ticehurst, 84, 86, 97, 102.

Messrs Tilley & Co. (Antiques) Ltd, 120, 289.

G. Tinsley Esq., 69–70.

Tuke Collection, 328.

Messrs J. & E. D. Vandekar, 34.

Victoria and Albert Museum (Crown copyright) I, J, 55, 103, 133, 151, 156, 183, 216, 221, 235, 247, 257, 285, 288, 313, 331, 337, 359, 373, 378, 393, 442, 447, 451–52, 508–9, 519, 555.

S. A. Vine Esq., 294, 302–3.

Messrs James Waring (Brighton), 39, 322, 450.

Waring's Masterpieces . . . of the 1862 Exhibition, 304.

Messrs Josiah Wedgwood & Sons Ltd, 505.

B. White Esq., 361–62.

A. Woods Esq., 173, 177, 181, 185.

Worcester Royal Porcelain Co. Ltd (Dyson Perrins Museum), G, 96, 110, 295, 299–300, 518, 525, 534–36, 552, 557, 567.

Worthing Museum, 407.

In addition, some collectors have expressed a wish that their names not be recorded, a wish that I must respect. The following illustrations are of objects in such private collections: 68, 209, 225, 277, 289, 334, 357, 397, 412–13, 418, 431–32, 437–38, 445, 472, 524, 531, 546.

To complete the list of photograph sources, I must record that the following Plates are of objects in my own possession: F, 1–2, 23, 32, 76–78, 87–88, 90, 94, Colour Plate II, 125, 155, 157, 160, 162, 169, 171, 190–91, 193–94, 211, 272–74, 276,

278, 283, 319, 341–43, 345, 352–53, 368, 377, 379–81, 386, 390, 405–6, Colour Plate VIII, 551, 553–54, 558.

Apart from the persons who have so kindly lent me objects or permitted their objects to be photographed and displayed in this book, I am also most grateful to the several photographers who have been responsible for the posing and taking of the photographs, especially John Beckerley, C. H. Cannings, Derek Gardiner.

Geoffrey A. Godden,
19A Crescent Road,
Worthing, Sussex,
England.

Introduction

This book is concerned solely with porcelain (the companion volume on British Pottery deals with the other, non-porcelain wares). Unlike earthenware, porcelain is translucent to varying degrees when held to the light. The Chinese distinguished the two by the clear, pure ring of porcelain as opposed to the dull sound of earthenware.

British porcelains cannot pre-date the 1740s and most found today are of nineteenth-century origin, although some owners fondly believe their family pieces to be three hundred or more years old. Such owners believe that age adds to the value of a piece, but this is not necessarily so, for age in itself is not a virtue! I do not wish to become involved in a discussion of commercial values, but it should be stated that a fine-quality Victorian object is of greater worth than a poor eighteenth-century item.

The products of the main British porcelain factories are illustrated in alphabetical order in the following main section of this book, but it will be helpful first to make various basic points.

Firstly, great emphasis should be laid on the characteristic shapes, for by the close study of these forms most articles can be attributed. I must repeat *close study*, for to many people the teapots shown in Plates A–D will be deemed the same, though they differ in one or more important respect. If you are prepared to compare closely the shapes of articles awaiting identification with the illustrations featured in this book you will be able to identify a mass of unmarked British porcelain, but if to you every teapot with a spout and handle is identical then no book or advice will be of help.

Little reliance should be placed on the pattern, for a popular pattern, or style, was very often copied by several manufacturers. The colourful 'Japan' patterns are by no means confined to the Derby factory, and probably the Coalport factory in the 1800–1830 period produced more of these so-called Derby patterns than did the Derby management. Similarly, the Minton factory made more floral-encrusted Coalport-styled porcelains than did the Shropshire factory.

However, patterns can be helpful when the pattern-number matches that known to be related to the pattern at a given factory. For example, the pattern shown in Plate E is normally a Worcester one, but when it occurs as in this case, with the pattern-number 66, it will be a Minton example, as is proved by a study of the Minton pattern-books. The number 1624 will indicate a Spode origin for the same design. In the captions to the illustrations the pattern-number will be cited when it occurs, and some pages from factory pattern-books are illustrated. It should be noted here that pattern-numbers will not appear separated from a factory-mark before 1790.

Plate A Chamberlain-Worcester.

Plate B Flight-Worcester.

Plate C New Hall.

Plate D John Rose, Coalport.

Plate E

The basic type and range of pattern-numbers can also be very helpful, for while most factories started with straightforward numbering from 1 to 1000, several then commenced a new series, expressed in fractional form, 2/100, 2/101, etc., or with a letter prefix such as B.100, while others such as Spode continued in a simple form 1001, 1002, etc. An object bearing the pattern-number 2/789 cannot, therefore, be of Spode manufacture. As each factory is discussed in the main section the range of pattern-numbers where known will be cited. The following is a brief summary of the basic systems favoured by the main firms after the number 1000 had been reached.

Simple progressive numbers

Anstice, Horton & Rose (of Coalport).
Chamberlain-Worcester.
Copeland & Garrett.
Daniels.
Davenports.
Grainger-Worcester—up to number 2000 of *c.* 1845.
Herculaneum.
Masons.
Mintons—up to about 1850, after which letter prefixes were employed.
New Hall.
Ridgway—dessert and dinner wares only.
Rockingham—up to about 1559. A few later patterns are fractional under the number 2.
Spode.

Fractional pattern-numbers

Coalport (John Rose & Co.).
Grainger-Worcester—after about the year 1845.

Ridgway—tea wares expressed under number 2, later under 5 (see page 365).
Rockingham—a few late patterns were expressed under the number 2.

Letter prefix

Copelands—after number 9999 had been reached *c.* 1852.
Grainger-Worcester—prefix G used on late range after about 1870.
Mintons—after about 1850.

This book is not really concerned with marks, although some are illustrated or noted in the captions. Nevertheless, marks can be most helpful, and as far as the nineteenth-century wares are concerned they are a reliable[1] indication of origin, and very many pieces made after 1870 can be dated to the year, and often even to the month, of manufacture, by reference to the manufacturer's date-cypher which was often added to the standard mark. The key to these date codes for Royal Crown Derby, Royal Worcester, and Minton porcelains will be found in my *Encyclopaedia of British Pottery and Porcelain Marks* (Barrie & Jenkins, London, 1964) with details of some four thousand British ceramic marks. The more usual basic marks are also listed in the smaller *Handbook of British Pottery and Porcelain Marks* (Barrie & Jenkins, London, 1968) but it will be helpful to list here my basic rules for dating marks.

Printed marks incorporating the Royal Arms are of nineteenth- or twentieth-century date.

Printed marks incorporating the *name of the pattern* are subsequent to 1810, and often much later.

Marks incorporating the word 'Limited' or the abbreviations 'Ltd', etc., denote a date after 1861 and most examples are much later.

Marks incorporating the words 'Trade Mark' are subsequent to the Act of 1862.

Inclusion of the word 'Royal' in a firm's title or trade name suggests a date in the second half of the nineteenth century, or often a twentieth-century date.

Use of the word 'England' denotes a date after 1891 (although some manufacturers added the name at a slightly earlier date).

The term 'Made in England' is purely a twentieth-century one.

The words 'Bone China' or 'English Bone China' also indicate a twentieth-century date.

Dates incorporated in a mark should *not* be regarded as the period of manufacture. In most cases such dates refer to the establishment of the firm or of its predecessors.

Differing methods of manufacture can also be very helpful, and in several cases characteristics are pointed out in the captions, but here I wish to discuss briefly the two basic methods of moulding.

Non-circular objects which could not be formed on the potter's wheel were normally formed in moulds. All figures and groups would be moulded, and the difference between the two basic methods of moulding can be of great assistance in correctly attributing an example.

---

[1] The 'Swansea' and 'Nantgarw' marks have been copied on later products and Samson hard-paste copies of Derby porcelain can bear the mark of the original. The gold-anchor Chelsea mark should always be treated with caution (see page 119).

Plate F

The first method is called 'press-moulding', in which the soft porcelain body was pressed into moulds for the different component parts of the whole—the head, legs and arms, body, etc., being formed initially as separate units, which were then built up by a 'repairer' to form the whole. Such 'press-moulded' examples are relatively heavy, and if one can see inside the base, it will appear uneven, with finger-marks showing how the clay was pressed into the mould and, if broken, the walls will show uneven thickness. See the illustration Plate F of the broken Bow figure.

The following porcelain producers made press-moulded figures:

Bow (some very rare examples may have been produced from slip-casting moulds),

Bristol,
Plymouth,
Worcester.

The second method is called 'slip-casting'. Here, the liquid porcelain, or 'slip', is poured into plaster-of-Paris moulds which absorb some of the surplus moisture, forming a wall of uniform thickness, before the surplus slip is poured from the mould. Such cast figures are lighter in weight than the press-moulded examples, and where the inside of the figure is visible, it will appear smooth, with walls of even thickness. A projection on the outside will appear on the inside as an indentation. Unfortunately, the bases which were added at a later stage very often prohibit the collector from examining the inside, although this is sometimes possible through the vent-hole left in most bases.

The following eighteenth-century English porcelain producers employed the slip-casting method, but it should be remembered that reproductions and all nineteenth- and twentieth-century figures were made in this now-standard manner:

Chelsea,
Derby,
'Girl in a Swing'-class,
Liverpool (Gilbody factory),
Longton Hall.

The late Arthur Lane gave the impression in his excellent *English Porcelain Figures of the 18th Century* (Faber & Faber, London, 1961) that the slip-cast figures were formed in their complete state: 'When figures were made by the slip-casting process, the assembled moulds were often inverted . . . the slip poured in through a fair-sized circular hole in what would be the underside of the base. . . .' I consider this to be a gross over-simplification, and it seems obvious that many intricate pieces

19

could not have been cast in one piece, the same assembling technique being employed as with the press-moulded pieces. In fact, even today, British slip-cast figures and groups are made in separate pieces and assembled to form the whole. The illustration Plate G shows the component parts of a slip-cast Royal Worcester bull model.

The collector should note that, nearly always, the base was formed separately. Sometimes this fact can cause confusion, for the base may show signs of being press-moulded, whereas the figure itself is slip-cast. Some Longton Hall figures fall into this category, as do some Derby figures and groups. The reader should also bear in mind that a head or neck (often seen on broken figures) may appear solid even if slip-cast, and press-moulded arms and legs will nearly always be solid. In some cases, the body of a Bow figure is completely solid.

Brief chronological survey

Prior to the 1740s the only porcelains readily available in the British Isles were the Chinese and Japanese porcelains imported in the vessels of the British East India Company, for the importing of the early Continental wares was prohibited. This trade in Oriental ware was very large, and the standard articles were sold in London, by auction, to the leading dealers, who subsequently divided the large wholesale lots into smaller parcels which were resold to retailers from all parts of the country. Much was also re-exported, large quantities to Ireland and some even to North America.

It was this popular Oriental porcelain[1] that the English porcelain manufacturers were striving to copy when they succeeded in producing their own version of the white, semi-translucent porcelain body. They were also influenced to some degree by the porcelains that had earlier been introduced on the Continent, in France and Germany, although at first such Sèvres and Dresden (Meissen) porcelains were known only to the nobility and were not on general sale. The early English porcelains were similar to the Oriental in general appearance, but the two were vastly different in make-up. The Oriental was what we now call 'true' or 'hard-paste' porcelain, requiring only one firing, whereas the English was of the artificial or 'soft-paste' type, requiring one firing before the glaze was applied, and another after glazing. We are not here concerned with a chemical analysis of the different porcelains, but it must be clearly understood that the English artificial porcelains and covering glazes are relatively warm and 'friendly' to the touch and that the overglaze enamel colours tend to sink into the glaze slightly, mellowing with it. Where a break or chip exposes the porcelain body the texture is slightly granular.

In contrast, the 'hard-paste' or 'true' porcelains tend to appear cold and glittery, the enamel colours showing less tendency to sink into the glaze. They look and feel hard, as they are, and a fracture will normally run in facets—as with glass. The body shows a slightly glazed effect owing to its vitrification at the high firing temperature.

Having said that the Continental wares are 'hard-paste' and the British, 'soft-paste', we must qualify this general statement. Some early French and Italian are soft-paste and some English porcelains are of the hard-paste variety. While we can disregard here the soft-paste Continental wares of Sèvres and other factories, we must note that the English Bristol (c. 1770–81) and Plymouth (c. 1768–70) porcelains are hard and that the later New Hall wares of the 1781–1812 period are of the same type, although the products of the latter factory could hardly be

---

[1] The story of these Oriental wares is discussed at length in my book titled *Chinese Export Market Porcelains*.

mistaken for Continental porcelains. We must also note that during the 1790–1810 period some English factories including Coalport were using what is technically a hard-paste porcelain, but in shape, style of decoration, and thickness of potting such wares would not be mistaken for Oriental or Continental porcelains.

Having explained that the mid-eighteenth-century English manufacturers were modelling their wares on the Oriental porcelains which had by then firmly established the market and set the fashion—especially for porcelains decorated in underglaze-blue—we can proceed to show the chronological sequence of events relating to the development of British porcelains and pinpoint some landmarks.

1745

CHELSEA While we have as yet no positive evidence for the date of establishment of the famous Chelsea factory, it was clearly in existence in 1745 as this date is found on some 'Chelsea'-marked jugs. (See below.) This factory continued until 1769, after which it was taken over by the Derby management and produced what we term 'Chelsea-Derby' porcelain. Typical Chelsea porcelains are featured in Plates 116–44, and in general the porcelains are the richest of the English eighteenth-century wares and those best able to rival products of the leading Continental factories.

Plate H

1747–8

LIMEHOUSE   The *Daily Advertiser* of January 1st 1747 contained an announcement relating to the new ware on sale at Dick's Store, Limehouse on the banks of the Thames. However, by May 1748 "All the Goods in Trade of the Limehouse manufactory, commonly called English China . . ." were being sold. The wares formerly attributed to William Reid of Liverpool — as Plate 319 — were on the evidence of finds on the site early in 1990 produced at Limehouse.

Plate I

1749

BRISTOL The earliest Bristol porcelain was *not* hard-paste, but an attractive soft-paste containing soap rock, talc, or magnesia. The small works was established by Benjamin Lund and William Miller in 1749, but in 1752 the concern was 'united with the Worcester Porcelain Company where for the future the whole business will be carried on'.

1749

LONGTON HALL In or about 1749 William Jenkinson established at Longton Hall what is believed to be the first porcelain manufactory in the Staffordshire Potteries. One of the partners—William Littler—is normally associated with this factory, and after the closure in 1760 Littler went to West Pans in Scotland where he continued to deal in, and decorate, Longton Hall porcelain.

1750

DERBY Again, like Bow, we have no precise information on the date of foundation of the Derby factory, but certain white jugs appear with the initial D and the date 1750 (see below). Although some experimental pieces may have been made in the late 1740s, the still-flourishing Derby ceramic tradition is generally considered to have begun in the 1750s.

Plate J

1751

WORCESTER The long and interesting story of porcelain manufacture in Worcester starts in June 1751 when a long article of agreement between fifteen subscribers, including Dr John Wall and William Davis, was signed. As most readers well know, the Worcester Royal Porcelain Company is today still producing superb-quality wares.

1753

VAUXHALL (London). The potter John Sanders with Nicholas Crisp (a jeweller) produced porcelains at Vauxhall between May 1753 and 1764. Excavations on the site have suggested that the porcelains previously attributed to William Ball of Liverpool (see Plates 315-318) were made at Vauxhall.

1757

LOWESTOFT Here in the small fishing port of Lowestoft on the extreme East Coast of England was established in 1757 a modest porcelain factory. The early wares, before the 1770s, are painted only in underglaze-blue, and in general the factory catered only for the local trade.

1768

HARD-PASTE PORCELAIN At Plymouth in 1768 the first-known English true, or hard-paste, porcelain was made, between 1768 and 1770. Its manufacture was continued at Bristol during the 1770–81 period.

1775

CAUGHLEY The Caughley or 'Salopian' porcelain factory was established in 1775, on the site of an earlier pottery. Its soapstone body is very similar to that employed at the Worcester factory, and Worcester shapes and patterns were sometimes copied.

c. 1789

BONE CHINA At about this period Josiah Spode reputedly produced the first bone china, which was to become, early in the nineteenth century, the standard body for English porcelain. Today fine English porcelain is widely called 'bone china' although this name has only been adopted in the present century—Spode did not openly use the term.

Calcined animal (or fish) bone was used at Bow in the 1740s and it formed a part of many eighteenth-century ceramic bodies. However, Spode's new porcelains of the 1790s contained no less than 50% bone ash, with 25% Cornish stone and 25% china clay. This compact white body is stronger than most true or hard-paste porcelains, but its firing at approximately 1260°C presents some difficulty due to the comparatively narrow margin of error.

For all practical purposes, it can be said that all English table wares of the post-1815 period are bone china.

1790s

The introduction of bone china by Spode in about 1789 was well timed, for in the 1790s the amount of Chinese porcelain imported into the British Isles was cut by the heavy duties then being levied, a duty that rose to over 100% in 1799. By that time the English East India Company had ceased the importation of Chinese porcelains—wares that had been pouring into the country throughout the eighteenth century. This encouraged numerous potters to produce refined porcelain, and several small concerns sought to take advantage of the situation.

In part, at least, the successful establishment of the following porcelain works in the 1780s and 1790s is due to the tailing-off of the importation of Chinese ceramics, which left the market open for the new manufacturers: Chamberlain, Coalport, Davenport, Grainger, Masons, Minton, and Pinxton. Most later firms also indirectly profited from the end of the main import of the once-popular Chinese porcelains—the main rival of the earlier porcelain manufacturers.[1]

1790s

OVAL TEAPOTS From about this date, the old traditional globular form of teapot gave way to those of an approximate oval plan. While some New Hall teapots of the shapes shown in Plates 407 and 410 may be of a slightly earlier period, no oval teapot will pre-date 1790.

1796

PINXTON The first trial pieces were fired in April 1796. John Coke and William Billingsley (from the Derby factory) established the works. The products in body, glaze, and decoration closely follow the Derby porcelains, except that no figures are recorded and pieces are functional rather than ornamental.

[1] Some Chinese porcelain continued to be imported as 'Private Trade', the concern of the ships' officers and crew.

1796

COALPORT By at least August 1796 the porcelain works of Rose, Blakeway & Rose (Rose & Co.) were established near the banks of the River Severn at Coalport (only a few miles from the Caughley factory). A further factory worked by Messrs Anstice, Horton & Rose was also situated at Coalport (see page 149).

1797

MINTON In May 1796 Thomas Minton's pottery at Stoke-on-Trent commenced production of earthenwares. In the following year, porcelain was made as well and was subsequently to become the most important of the firm's varied products. Fine bone china bearing the famous Minton name is still made today.

1800

HERCULANEUM In 1796 the Herculaneum factory was established at Liverpool. The staple products were fine earthenwares and stoneware-type bodies, but porcelain was introduced in about 1800.

1826

ROCKINGHAM In 1826 the commercial production of porcelain was started at the so-called Rockingham Works at Swinton in Yorkshire. Porcelain was only one of the products, and for many years previously fine-quality earthenwares had been made there by the Bramelds.

Much confusion arises over unmarked Rockingham-type wares, and in several instances tea wares will be shown in this book which to the amateur appear to be Rockingham but which were made by other factories following the general taste of the 1830–40 period.

1842

REGISTRATION OF DESIGN From 1842 until 1883 manufactured designs—not only in pottery and porcelain—could be protected from piracy by registration at the Patent Office in London. Each basic design was allocated a diamond-shaped mark, the various letters and numerals in the inner four angles being unique to each official entry. From such marks the day, month, and year of registration (not of manufacture) can be ascertained by reference to the following Table.

TABLE OF REGISTRATION-MARKS 1843–1883

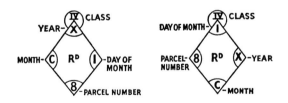

Above are the two patterns of Design Registration-Marks that were in current use between the years 1842 and 1883. Keys to year and month code-letters are given opposite.

The left-hand diamond was used during the years 1842 to 1867. A change was made in 1868, when the right-hand diamond was adopted.

INDEX TO YEAR- AND MONTH-LETTERS

YEARS

	1842–67		1868–83
	Year = Letter at Top		*Year = Letter at Right*

1842–67		1868–83	
A = 1845	N = 1864	A = 1871	L = 1882
B = 1858	O = 1862	C = 1870	P = 1877
C = 1844	P = 1851	D = 1878	S = 1875
D = 1852	Q = 1866	E = 1881	U = 1874
E = 1855	R = 1861	F = 1873	V = 1876
F = 1847	S = 1849	H = 1869	W = (1–6 March)
G = 1863	T = 1867	I = 1872	1878
H = 1843	U = 1848	J = 1880	X = 1868
I = 1846	V = 1850	K = 1883	Y = 1879
J = 1854	W = 1865		
K = 1857	X = 1842		
L = 1856	Y = 1853		
M = 1859	Z = 1860		

MONTHS (BOTH PERIODS)

A = December

B = October

C or O = January

D = September

E = May

G = February

H = April

I = July

K = November (and December 1860)

M = June

R = August (and 1–19 September 1857)

W = March

Quite apart from discovering the earliest possible date of any piece bearing this form of mark, the mark also enables the student to discover, by reference to the official files, the name of the manufacturer. This can be of great interest, for the products of several firms which did not employ a factory imprint can be traced by means of the registration-mark. The section on the porcelains of Messrs Samuel Alcock & Co. (Plates 1–14) illustrates well the helpfulness of the registration-mark.

It must be stated that this mark does not prove a British origin, for some Continental manufacturers and retailers registered their designs in London.

1844

PARIAN By 1844 (or 1842) the matt white, porcelain-type body which was later termed 'Parian' was introduced by Messrs Copeland & Garrett and by other firms such as Mintons. The early examples, such as the 1846 copy of John Gibson's 'Narcissus' shown in Plate K, are often of very fine quality, but the lesser firms in endeavouring to lower the price of their Parian reduced the quality and so tended to spoil the market. Being slightly translucent the Parian wares are featured in this volume in a special section—Plates 420–25.

Plate K

1847

W. T. COPELAND In 1847 W. T. Copeland succeeded the partnership of Copeland & Garrett (1833–47) to continue the old Spode tradition at the original factory at Stoke. This firm continued until 1970, when the trading style was changed to 'Spode Limited'.

1862

ROYAL WORCESTER On 24 June 1862 R. W. Binns, on the retirement of his former partner W. H. Kerr (of Messrs Kerr & Binns, 1852–62), formed a new company called The Worcester Royal Porcelain Company. This firm and its products are familiarly known as 'Royal Worcester', and the company continues to this day producing superb-quality wares at Worcester.

1870

PÂTE-SUR-PÂTE This technique of cameo-like work on porcelain (or rather on tinted Parian) was introduced in France, but in 1870 M. L. Solon came to Stoke-on-Trent and introduced this expensive and painstaking form of decoration to Mintons. Subsequently he trained apprentices, and several other firms produced pâte-sur-pâte pieces. A special section is devoted to this class of ware. (See Plates 426–34.)

1876

DERBY In 1876 a new company was established in Derby under the title 'Derby Crown Porcelain Company'. This was not directly related to the old factory. In January 1890 Queen Victoria appointed this firm 'Manufacturers of Porcelain to Her Majesty', and from then to the present day the trading title has been 'The Royal Crown Derby Porcelain Company'.

1884

REGISTRATION-NUMBERS A simple progressive system of design-registration came into being in January 1884, to replace the old diamond-shaped device (see page 26). Such official numbers are normally prefixed 'R^d N^o'. The period of registration can be gauged by reference to the following Table.

DESIGN-REGISTRATION NUMBERS FOUND ON WARES FROM 1884

(These numbers are normally prefixed by 'R^d N^o', and were registered between 1 January and 31 December of the year stated.)

Numbers	Year	Numbers	Year
1 – 19753	1884	291241 – 311657	1897
19754 – 40479	1885	311658 – 331706	1898
40480 – 64519	1886	331707 – 351201	1899
64520 – 90482	1887	351202 – 368153	1900
90483 – 116647	1888	368154 – 385087	1901
116648 – 141263	1889	385088 – 402912	1902
141273 – 163762	1890	402913 – 424016	1903
163767 – 185712	1891	424017 – 447547	1904
185713 – 205239	1892	447548 – 471485	1905
205240 – 224719	1893	471486 – 493486	1906
224720 – 246974	1894	493487 – 518414	1907
246975 – 268391	1895	518415 – 534962	1908
268392 – 291240	1896		

For a continuation of this Table to 1987 the reader is referred to Geoffery Godden's *Encyclopaedia of British Porcelain Manufacturers* (Barrie & Jenkins, London, 1988).

Alcock

SAMUEL ALCOCK & CO.
(c. 1828–59)

THE FRONT VIEW OF MESS.ᴿˢ SAMUEL ALCOCK & Cᵒˢ CHINA MANUFACTORY, BURSLEM.

Between 1828 and 1859 Messrs Samuel Alcock & Co. produced a vast amount of high-quality porcelain (which was normally unmarked) as well as various types of earthenware. The partnership owned a factory at Cobridge until 1853 as well as the famous Hill Pottery at Burslem, so that both place-names, Cobridge and Burslem, occur in the marks employed.

In the 1833 Government report on conditions of employment for children, the inspector reported that Alcock's 'Porcelain and China Works' employed four hundred persons. He also observed that 'here were forty-two painters in one room, a greater number than I had before observed in one apartment, one third of them were adult males. . . .' Some six years later John Ward in his *The Borough of Stoke-upon-Trent* (W. Lewis & Son, London, 1843) spoke about the Alcock concern, placing it second to that of Enoch Wood & Son (page 413).

'Next in importance are the China and Earthenware Works of Samuel Alcock & Co., who occupy three sets of pot-works near together, situate at the Hill-top, viz., a large manufactory built by the late J. & R. Riley, on the site of John Taylor's house and works; another considerable manufactory, late the house and works of John Robinson & Sons; and another adjacent, formerly William Taylor's house and works. In these manufactories, three of the better sort of houses of the last century are absorbed, or have been swept away, to make room for buildings of trade.

The productions of Messrs. Alcock & Co., in ornamental china, are of a first-rate description, consisting of table and tea-services, enriched with exquisite landscape paintings and other devices; of vases, fancy bouquettes, articles of toilette, and elaborately modelled subjects from history and romance in biscuit china. Whilst this article is in the press [1839] Mr. Alcock has completed the rebuilding of the front of his manufactory which presents the most striking and ornamental object of its kind within the precincts of the Borough. [This 1839 engraving is reproduced.] . . . Messrs. Alcock & Co. are largely engaged in the export trade to America.'

This contemporary account laid stress on the 'elaborately modelled subjects . . . in biscuit china', and this aspect of the Alcock productions was referred to in retrospect in the *Art Union* magazine of December 1846:

'Some years ago this manufactory seemed likely to outstrip all its rivals in the excellence of its miniature statuary, having then the valuable assistance of an artist of great ability as a sculptor. . . .'

This 1846 account refers to the Italian Giovanni Meli (born *c.* 1815), who subsequently worked for Messrs Copeland & Garrett. Later on, he worked on his own account and for other firms. A typical and early Alcock portrait-bust is shown in Plate 1, with the printed mark on the reverse shown in Plate 2. Other busts in this series have a glazed plinth—sometimes with gilt enrichments, as the two featured in the *Illustrated Encyclopaedia of British Pottery and Porcelain* (Plate 12). Similar biscuit—that is, unglazed—china busts were made by Messrs Copeland & Garrett, by Mintons, and by the Rockingham concern.

The matt white biscuit porcelain was a great feature of the Alcock factories. The standing figure shown in Plate 3 is probably the finest example ever to have been made in this body in the nineteenth century—it probably represents the famous Austrian dancer Fanny Ellsler (1810–84)—and the detail and sharpness of the modelling cannot be fully seen in any reproduction. As the biscuit china gave way to the more creamy Parian body in the 1840s, Messrs Alcock & Co. produced a wide range of Parian wares, including many well-designed jugs. The firm's wares shown at the 1851 Exhibition included many ornamental jugs, cups, vases, figures, and groups in the Parian body. These 1851 exhibits were catalogued as being modelled by Alfred Crowquill, S. W. Arnold, and Samuel Giovanni. The latter reference may relate to Giovanni Meli, who had by then left the firm. While much of the Parian ware and the earlier biscuit china was unmarked, some examples bear a printed Royal Arms mark with the name added below. The Parian jug illustrated in Plate 14 shows this mark under the base. Other pieces may bear the initial-mark S.A. & Co.

While the biscuit china and the later Parian was sometimes marked, as was some of the earthenware, the Alcock porcelains—especially the table wares—are very seldom marked, and as yet the useful porcelains of the 1828–43 period have not been identified. The quality and range of the post-1842 pieces can be gauged by the fact that some basic shapes were registered and bear the diamond-shaped registration-mark (see page 26). The porcelains shown in Plates 4–10 illustrate some of these basic Alcock shapes, bearing a range of typical decorations—including floral-encrusted work. The reader will see that some of the vases and tea wares are in the style so often attributed to the Rockingham factory, and much Alcock porcelain is incorrectly called Rockingham. However, the known Alcock pattern-numbers are very high, running into several thousands (such as 9782), and are often in fractional form ($\frac{2}{5777}$, for example). These are numbers that are clearly not related to the Rockingham series (see page 376).

By the time of the 1851 Exhibition, Elizabeth Alcock, Samuel's widow, was running the pottery with the help of her two sons, Samuel and Thomas. At this period the factory was a large and important one, employing nearly seven hundred persons. Unfortunately, the functional table wares shown at the 1851 Exhibition are not described in the official catalogue, which includes only basic entries such as 'Series of porcelain desserts', 'Series of porcelain table ware', 'Series of porcelain tea ware'. The firm's reluctance to mark such porcelains has resulted in the Alcock porcelains being little known and unjustly neglected.

In 1860 Alcock's Hill Pottery at Burslem was taken over by Sir James Duke & Nephews, who continued the Alcock tradition until 1866. These later porcelains are sometimes marked with an impressed hand device. The contemporary engraving reproduced below illustrates some of their products as shown at the 1862 Exhibition.

For further information the reader is referred to Dr and Mrs G. Barnes' contribution to *Staffordshire Porcelain* (Granada, 1983), chapter 21.

1 A typical Samuel Alcock 'biscuit'-porcelain portrait-bust. 9 inches high. Published in 1828.

2 The back view of the bust illustrated left, showing the printed mark with date of publication.

3 A superb-quality Samuel Alcock 'biscuit'-porcelain figure of Fanny Ellsler. The model is by S. W. Arnold and was shown at the 1851 Exhibition. 14½ inches high. S.A. initial-mark with bee-hive device, see Plate 2.

5 A pair of blue-ground Alcock vases, showing front and back views. The basic shape registered on 21 February 1843 9¾ inches high. Printed registration-mark, pattern 2/3487.

6 A set of three Alcock vases, the basic shape as Plate 5, but with encrusted flowers. 9¾ and 9 inches high. Printed registration-mark, pattern 2/5777.

opposite page
4 A Samuel Alcock tea set in the so-called Rockingham style, the basic shapes registered on 14 June 1843. Green, buff, and gold. Teapot 7½ inches high. Printed diamond-shaped registration-mark (see page 26) on teapot.

7 A floral-encrusted Alcock vase, the basic shape registered on 20 February 1844. 10 inches high. Printed registration-mark.

8 Four green-ground, scenic-panelled Alcock porcelain vases of a type often attributed to the Rockingham factory, although the pattern-number could not relate to that factory. The basic shape registered in 1844. 11 and 10 inches high. Pattern-number 2/6153.

9 An Alcock porcelain basket of fine quality, the relief-moulded border design registered in January 1855. 9 inches long. Printed registration-mark.

10 A scenic-painted Alcock dessert service, the basic shapes being registered on 6 January 1855. The border is yellow and blue, but many different painted designs may be found. Printed registration-mark. Pattern-number 3/7195.

11 A black-ground Alcock Etruscan-style porcelain vase. 11¾ inches high. Initial-mark S.A. & Co. Pattern-number 6422. *c.* 1840.

12 & A Alcock's 'Royal Patriotic Jug', both sides being shown. This printed design was registered in December 1845. 7¼ inches high.

13 An Alcock printed porcelain jug, showing the fractional pattern-number and initial-mark. 7½ inches high. *c.* 1850.

14 An Alcock, moulded Parian jug—one of many such jugs—showing the Royal Arms name-mark. 9 inches high. *c.* 1850.

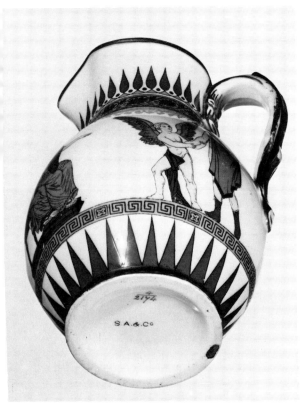

Belleek

The date of establishment of this factory is not known for certain, several authorities give dates in the 1850s, but 1863 would seem more accurate. An account of the Belleek products in the 1865 Dublin Exhibition mentions that it was then of 'quite recent introduction', having begun 'about two years ago'.

This early account is of great interest and extracts are here quoted.

M'Birney & Armstrong. Belleek. Co. Fermanagh.
Table and toilet ware in stone china, stoneware, mortars &c, for chemical purposes; Parian china figures, statuettes &c and earthenware.
This branch of manufacturing industry is of quite recent introduction into Ireland. . . . about two years ago they began to manufacture the ordinary useful classes of goods for table and toilet purposes; and the visitors to the Dublin exhibition of 1865 had the opportunity of seeing the aptitude of the children for the pottery trade by the skill and dexterity evinced by the Belleek youth, who during the exhibition were daily engaged in making jugs etc.
The Belleek pottery at present employs about 70 hands of which number about 30 are boys and girls learning the different branches of making ware. . . .
We were induced since the close of the Exhibition, to visit the Belleek factory in the Co. Fermanagh, and found there, after a most careful investigation occupying some days, that the Pottery, now only in its infancy . . . will beyond all doubt, take a prominent position amongst the manufacturers of Great Britain. . . . At the time of our visit, we found that not only were there large quantities of goods sent off daily to the different towns in England and Ireland . . . but the orders on the books from the United States, Canada and Australia far exceeding what (of necessity) the limited resources of the factory could supply.

The above account obviously shows the situation a few years after the establishment of the Belleek factory in, or about, 1863. Its establishment at this location, far removed from other centres, was due to the discovery of beds of felspar on the estate. This material was apparently sent to Worcester for trial and was found to be highly suitable for porcelain manufacture. As a result, Robert William Armstrong formed a partnership with David McBirney, trading for the most part as D. McBirney & Co. Workmen were brought over from Staffordshire, including several persons from the works of W. H. Goss (see page 246), but at first mostly utilitarian objects were made, as the above account of the 1865 Exhibition shows.

41

By at least September 1868 the now-familiar, ornately moulded, ornamental forms were being produced, as is shown by the registered designs which date from this period. These traditional Belleek forms were very often modelled on marine subjects, and these wares were designed by Mr and Mrs Armstrong. Llewellynn Jewitt, writing shortly before 1878, noted, 'The chief peculiarities of the ornamental goods produced at Belleek are, its lightness of body, its rich, delicate, cream-like, or ivory tint, and the glittering iridescence of its glaze . . . an idea of which can only be given by recalling the beautiful hues of a highly-polished mother-of-pearl shell.' The attractive, warm-looking glaze is perhaps seen to the best advantage when it is contrasted with the unglazed Parian body.

The Belleek factory continues to the present day and has over a long period of time produced models originally introduced in the nineteenth century. In order to show a wide range of traditional shapes, sample pages from the firm's 1904 catalogue have been reproduced in Plates 17–21. Among the most celebrated Belleek products are the wonderfully light and delicate, interwoven porcelain baskets. These are so fine that one wonders how they could ever have been made, and once made how they have remained perfect over the years. The standard shapes are here shown in the reproduction of a 1923 advertisement (Plate 22), which also shows the standard trade-mark.

Engravings of Victorian Belleek are incorporated in Jewitt's *Ceramic Art of Great Britain* (1878 and 1883 editions, revised 1972 edition published by Barrie & Jenkins, London). Other examples are shown in my *Illustrated Encyclopaedia of British Pottery and Porcelain* and in C. and D. Shinn's *Illustrated Guide to Victorian Parian China* (Barrie & Jenkins, London, 1971). Special books include *Belleek* by Richard Degenhardt (Portfolio Press, U.S.A. 1978) and *An Illustrated Guide to Irish Belleek China* (E. Jay Lease, U.S.A. 1978).

The Belleek wares have been very popular in North America over a long period, and several American firms use the name Belleek in their own trade-marks—a point the collector should bear in mind. This is not to say that such wares are copies, although they are often in the style of the original.

15 Typical moulded Belleek tea wares based on marine subjects. Teapot 5¾ inches high. Early printed mark. *c.* 1875.

16 An unusual Belleek early-morning tea set on tray. Tray 14¾ × 12 inches. Printed mark. *c.* 1885.

opposite page
17 Ornamental Belleek wares, reproduced from the 1904 catalogue.

18 Belleek figure models, as shown in the 1904 catalogue.

19 Belleek ornamental wares, reproduced from the 1904 catalogue.

20 Belleek floral-encrusted *jardinières*, as shown in the 1904 catalogue.

21 Belleek jugs and vases, as shown in the 1904 catalogue.

22 A selection of openwork Belleek baskets, reproduced from a 1923 advertisement. Such examples are superbly potted and are almost unbelievably light. Each was built up by hand.

Bevington

JAMES AND JOHN BEVINGTON
(*c.* 1872–92)

A small selection of Bevington porcelains is featured, since the pieces often cause confusion and the mark appears to be little known. This mark comprises a copy of the Dresden crossed-swords with the monogram JB below.

The Bevington family specialised in the manufacture of Dresden-styled fancy porcelain; a typical advertisement of the period reads, 'James Bevington, Cobden Works, High Street, Hanley, Staffordshire, manufacturer of useful and ornamental fancy china. Raised flower goods, flower baskets, vases, centrepieces, table ornaments and every description of artistic china. . . .' The objects shown in Plates 23–26 are typical. The centre ornament in Plate 23 is engraved in James Bevington's advertisement of September 1880 (see below).

John Bevington used the crossed-swords and monogram-mark at the Kensington Works at Hanley, and the firm's duration was 1872–92, his products are often given an earlier date and are often attributed to other factories, such as Coalport, or even to the Dresden factory.

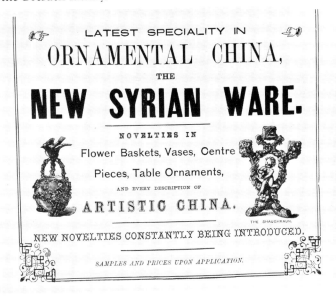

23 A pair of candlestick-figures by John Bevington of Hanley, with a candlestick by James Bevington. 10 inches high. *c.* 1881.

24 A pair of John Bevington's basket-figures after a Dresden original. The underglaze-blue mark is seen with the monogram J.B. 6½ inches high. *c.* 1880.

25 A pair of floral-encrusted John Bevington vases. Blue crossed-swords monogram-mark as seen in Plate 24. 9¼ inches high. *c.* 1885.

26 A pair of John Bevington figure flower-holders. Blue crossed-swords monogram-mark as seen in Plate 24. 7¼ inches high. *c.* 1885.

Bourne

CHARLES BOURNE, FOLEY POTTERIES
(*c.* 1807–30)

The Staffordshire porcelains produced by Charles Bourne are in one respect unique—they are marked with his initials, placed in fractional form over the pattern-number (see Plate 27). In other respects they rival in quality the more plentiful Spode or Ridgway porcelains of the 1810–20 period, and the porcelain is a compact bone china of good white tone, covered with a clear glaze, free from crazing. Some of the basic shapes are very similar to those employed at the two larger factories mentioned above, particularly those forms shown in Plates 28 and 30, while others (Plates 29, 31–34) are unique to the Bourne works. But always the quality is good and the products are well worth the study of collectors seeking unusual porcelains.

Charles Bourne represents one of many now little-known Staffordshire manufacturers who were turning out porcelains in the style of the leading manufacturers. If this potter had not chosen to mark his wares with his initials above the pattern-number, his products would be grouped with more fashionable names, and we would have no idea of the quality of the wares produced by some of these smaller firms. The term 'smaller' is comparative, for we have an interesting advertisement for the sale of his works in November 1830, which shows that there were six kilns and that the proprietor was a man of some standing. The advertisement which appeared in the *Staffordshire Sentinel* of 13 November 1830 reads:

CHINA AND EARTHENWARE

MANUFACTORY

AT THE FOLEY, NEAR LANE END

To be Let or Sold by Private contract, all these extensive and convenient premises consisting of three biscuit and three gloss ovens with hardening and enamelling kiln and kiln room to make thirty tons of clay a week. . . . Also, the very substantial dwelling-house, coach-house, stables and barn, with five acres of land, adjoining the canal company's railway with gardens, pleasure-ground, etc., complete, now in the possession of Mr. Charles Bourne, the proprietor, who is declining business on account of ill health. . . .

A reference to Charles Bourne as a manufacturer appears in the first available rate record in August 1807, but the marked porcelains would seem to date from about 1815 onwards (the vase shown as Plate 27 is of pattern-number 2), so that his earlier products could well have been confined to unmarked earthenwares. The reader is also referred to chapter 16 of *Staffordshire Porcelain*.

27 A Charles Bourne spill-vase showing under the base the typical initial-mark *cum* pattern-number. The number—in this case 2— being painted in fractional form below the identifying initials C B. All pieces subsequently featured in this section are marked in this manner. 4¾ inches high. *c.* 1807.

28 Part of a Charles Bourne 'Japan'-pattern tea set, showing typical shapes (the Ridgway firm made very similar forms) of the 1810–15 period. Pattern-number 287 below the initials C B.

29 A fine-quality Charles
Bourne dessert plate, with
relief-moulded border. Pattern
51. Diameter 8¾ inches. *c.* 1810.

30 A Charles Bourne dessert
dish, closely following a
standard Spode shape. Pattern-
number 202 under the initials
C B. 11½ × 7¼ inches. *c.* 1815.

31 A rare Charles Bourne vase of the 1815 period, bearing the initial-mark C B. 6¼ inches high.

32 A rare Charles Bourne cat, pattern-number 209 under the initials C B. 2½ inches high. *c.* 1815.

33 A Charles Bourne spill-vase of the 1815 period, pattern-number 367. 4½ inches high.

34 A fine-quality set of three Bourne porcelain spill-vases. Pattern-number 112 under the initials C B. Centre vase 6 inches high. *c.* 1810–15.

Bow

VARIOUS PARTNERSHIPS—
WEATHERBY & CROWTHER, FRYE & CO.
(*c.* 1747–76)

The so-called Bow porcelain factory was situated on the north side of Stratford High Street at Stratford Langthorne in the parish of West Ham in Essex, not directly at Bow on the Middlesex side of the Thames, although the porcelain has been and will always be termed 'Bow'.

Bow is one of the earliest of the English porcelain factories, being in operation at least by 1747. Three years before this a patent for the manufacture of porcelain had been taken out by Edward Heylyn and Thomas Frye, but as far as we know, no saleable porcelain was then produced by these partners. From about 1747 the active parties were John Weatherby and John Crowther.

The first recorded reference to the Bow wares occurs in Daniel Defoe's *Tour of Great Britain* (July 1748), which includes the following brief account:

> . . . the first village we come to is Bow where a large manufactory of porcelaine is lately set up. They have already made large quantities of tea cups, saucers, etc., which by some skilful persons are said to be little inferior to those brought from China. . . .

Here we see that the factory was in being and was producing modest useful wares. The comparison with the Chinese porcelains is interesting, as some small Bow inkpots of the 1750–51 period are inscribed 'Made at New Canton' (see page 23). The Bow porcelain body is vastly different from the true, or hard-paste, Chinese, but the soft-paste Bow porcelain is noteworthy for the inclusion of bone ash in its make-up, a fact which is helpful for identification (with the aid of chemical analysis). It can also be termed the father of English bone china (although the nineteenth-century bone china is a much whiter, more refined, product). In general, the Bow porcelain body is rather thickly potted and is not particularly translucent.

The rare, early Bow porcelain is of a very compact, almost creamy texture, which in the 1760s became more open or floury, with a slightly blued glaze. The early useful wares were often decorated in the Chinese manner with formal floral designs, and much was sold in the 'white', embellished only with applied floral sprigs in the style of the Fukien or 'Blanc-de-Chine' wares. Plate 39 illustrates both these typical styles. A large proportion of the useful wares were decorated in underglaze-blue, in the style of the imported Chinese 'Nankeen' wares. Some fine examples have a powder-blue ground (the speckled colour being achieved by blowing, or dusting, the powdered cobalt on the plate or dish, the white panels of which had previously been 'resisted' or covered). A typical powder-blue plate is shown in Plate 49, but similar examples were made at other factories such as Caughley, Lowestoft, and Worcester. Plates and dishes of this type are often marked with mock-Chinese characters (Plate 48) and one wonders if they were more saleable as Chinese rather than English wares. Certainly, to the eighteenth-century housewife buying her table china much of the Bow porcelain could well have been passed off as Oriental, and the example shown as Plate 50 was purchased recently from a dealer as being Chinese! In use, however, the Bow porcelain was not as durable as the Oriental, for the covering glaze was relatively soft, prone to staining—especially when it broke up into the network of fine hair-lines known as crazing—and tended to scratch and mark in use. The Bow plates and dishes were normally finished in the Chinese manner, without an applied foot-rim, the foot having only one angle (Plate 48).

Some rare Bow table wares were, like the Worcester porcelains, decorated with overglaze prints, and plates sometimes bore printed figure-designs. The tea bowl and saucer shown in Plate 54 is a quite rare, but attractive, example of this style of decoration. Some Chinese-styled figure patterns were achieved by adding a printed outline which was subsequently coloured in by cheap, semi-skilled labour. Printing in underglaze-blue was also carried out, but not on the scale favoured at Caughley or Worcester.

The Bow factory, over a period of nearly thirty years, produced a fine assortment of figures and groups, also roccoco-styled vases, sometimes encrusted with flowers (Plates 53 and 55). At first the figures were relatively simple, on low, flat bases, but in the 1760s the style became more florid with high scroll-bases and an ornate floral 'bocage' added behind the figure—a device which helped to support the figure during firing. Many of the Bow figures and groups have the square hole cut into the back (Plate 46), into which was sometimes set a metal branch, with a candle-holder or porcelain flowers, but this feature can occur on other examples, such as Derby. The Bow figures were normally press-moulded (page 18) and consequently they feel heavy for their size. Some were even solid. A selection of typical late figures is shown in Plates 56–63, but the reader is warned that hard-paste copies of some Bow pieces were made in France in the last century.

It is interesting to record that the Bow factory enjoyed close links with North America. It is believed that American clay was imported in the late 1740s and 1750s for use at the Bow factory, and subsequently much finished Bow porcelain was exported to America. There also seems to be a very close link with the American porcelain works of Bonnin & Morris in Philadelphia. This partnership's December 1769 advertisement observed that 'the clays of America are productive of as good porcelain as any heretofore manufactured at the famous factory in Bow near London and imported into the colonies and plantations. . . .' It is likely that some of the Bow employees were also attracted to this early American factory.

Little pre-1765 Bow porcelain is marked. An incised arrow-like device rarely occurs, and other early examples have an incised 'R' mark. The blue and white pieces often bear the painter's number or mock-Chinese marks (Plate 48), but in general the early enamelled table wares are not marked. After about 1765 a red-painted anchor-and-dagger device was often employed on both practical wares and figures. Sometimes workmen's marks in underglaze-blue can also occur. A typical example is reproduced in Plate 60.

The Bow factory closed in 1776 and it is often stated that William Duesbury of the Derby factory bought up the concern. However, there does not seem to be any evidence to substantiate this belief and the valuable figure moulds do not appear to have been re-used at Derby.

For further information on Bow porcelains the reader is recommended to consult Mr H. Tait's excellent catalogue of the 1959 exhibition of Bow porcelain held at the British Museum. Mr Tait is currently preparing a new work on these porcelains, which is to be published by Faber & Faber. In the meantime two general works contain good reviews of Bow porcelain: *English Blue & White Porcelain of the 18th century* by B. Watney (Faber & Faber, London, 1963) and *British Porcelain, 1745–1850*, edited by R. J. Charleston (E. Benn, London, 1965).

Two recent specialist books should be consulted: Anton Gabszewicz's *Bow Porcelain*, based on the Geoffrey Freeman collection (Lund Humphries, 1982) and Mrs Elizabeth Adams and Dr David Redstone's *Bow Porcelain* (Faber & Faber, 1981).

An interesting article by Elizabeth Adams is printed in *Apollo* magazine of January 1972. Information on the rare Bonnin & Morris American porcelains in the Bow style is given in an article by Graham Hood contained in *Antiques* magazine of June 1969. Further details of this American factory are given in Graham Hood's book *Bonnin and Morris of Philadelphia* (University of North Carolina Press, 1972).

35 A rare, early Bow porcelain tankard, showing in the enamelled decoration the influence of Chinese 'Famille Rose'-style porcelains. Unmarked. 5¼ inches high. *c.* 1750.

36 A Bow porcelain dish, the
enamelled design being copied
from the popular Oriental—in
this case, Japanese—
porcelains. $9\frac{3}{4} \times 10\frac{1}{4}$ inches.
c. 1755.

37 A selection of Bow sauce-
boats, showing in the
enamelled design and in the
relief-moulded sprigs the
influence of the Oriental wares,
although the basic shapes owe
more to European silver-forms.
c. 1750–55.

38 A relatively humble and originally inexpensive Bow cup in the style of the popular 'Blanc de Chine' porcelains. 2¼ inches high. *c.* 1755.

39 A typical Bow porcelain plate, showing the 'Blanc de Chine'-type sprig-motifs which were widely copied at Bow, with Chinese-style 'Famille Rose' enamelled decoration. The marriage of these two Oriental styles would not be found on Chinese plates. The glaze is rather crazed. 9½ inches. *c.* 1755–60.

40 A Bow, press-moulded figure of the actor Henry Woodward as the Fine Gentleman in *Lethe*. 10½ inches high. *c.* 1750–55.

41 The companion figure of Kitty Clive. Many figures of the 1745–55 period are found in the 'white', but some were originally embellished with unfired colour. 9¾ inches high. *c.* 1750–55.

42 A rare Bow porcelain group of the Chinese goddess Ki-Mao-Sao, after the painting by Watteau. The modelling of the female face is characteristic, as is the gilding, which is over a brown underlay. 10¼ inches long. *c.* 1755.

43 Two small Bow mugs or coffee-cans enamelled in a typical manner. 2½ inches high. *c.* 1755–60.

44 A fine, early pair of
enamelled Bow porcelain
cooks. Note the restrained
decoration in comparison with
later figures (Plates 61–63) and
the simple bases. 6¾ inches
high. *c.* 1755.

opposite page
47 A superb Bow water-bottle in the Oriental style, decorated in underglaze-blue. The granular ground is termed 'powder-blue'. $11\frac{1}{8}$ inches high. *c.* 1755–60.

45 A Bow figure, showing the influence of the Continental porcelains. Incised A F monogram. $6\frac{1}{2}$ inches high. *c.* 1755–60.

46 The reverse of a Bow figure, showing the square hole (for the fitment of a metal candle arm-branch) so often found on Bow figures and groups. 6 inches high. *c.* 1760.

48 The reverse of the Bow powder-blue plate in Plate 49, showing the Chinese form of foot-rim, and the mock-Chinese mark—in this case incorporating the Dresden crossed-swords device.

49 A typical Bow powder-blue plate (similar wares were made at other British factories) and a typical blue and white sauce-boat. Plate marked as Plate 48 above. Diameter 9 inches. *c.* 1755–60.

50 A rather heavy Bow blue and white plate, purchased from a dealer as Chinese! Foot as Plate 48. *c.* 1760.

51 A well-painted Bow blue and white plate of the woodman or Image pattern, showing to good effect the prevailing Oriental taste. Many fragments of this pattern were found on the factory-site. *c.* 1760.

52 Representative pieces of a Bow miniature, toy, or child's tea service, painted in underglaze-blue. Most eighteenth-century English factories made these charming miniature sets which are sometimes regarded as travellers' samples. This is clearly incorrect as in many cases the designs are unknown on full-size wares. See also Plates 90–91. *c.* 1760–65.

53 A rare two-piece Bow vase.
Unmarked. 9 inches high.
c. 1760.

54 A rare, red transfer-printed
Bow tea bowl and saucer
bearing a version of a print,
The Tea Party, better known on
Worcester wares. *c.* 1755–60.

opposite page
55 A typical Bow 'frill-vase' with mask-head handles. Encrusted with porcelain flowers and enamelled with insects. Unmarked. 11 inches high. *c.* 1760–65.

56 A Bow candlestick group (the candle-holder missing), showing rather heavy modelling and typical applied flowers and leaves. The base picked out in underglaze-blue. 8½ inches. *c.* 1760.

57 Three rare Bow porcelain bird or fowl models. The Chelsea factory made similar examples but the scroll base to the centre item is typical of the Bow pieces. Left-hand bird 7 inches high. *c.* 1755–60.

71

58 A pair of Bow musicians. The scroll bases are typical. 9½ and 9 inches high. *c.* 1760.

59 A set of Bow seated seasons. The scroll bases are typical. Anchor-and-dagger mark in red 6¼–6¾ inches high. *c.* 1760–65.

Colour Plate I A fine Bow candlestick-figure (one of a pair) with a large 'bocage' behind. The scroll base is typical, as are the touches of underglaze-blue on the candle-holder. Plate 60 shows the underside and marks. $9\frac{1}{2}$ inches high. *c.* 1765.

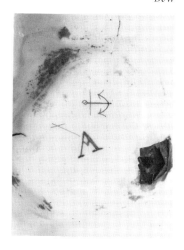

60 Detail of the base of the figure shown as Colour Plate I, illustrating the red-enamelled anchor-and-dagger mark, also in this case the initial A in underglaze-blue. This, or other initials, occurs on several Bow figures.

61 A pair of typical Bow figures of the 1760–65 period. The narrow spike-like leaves above the base should be noted. Anchor-and-dagger marks. $11\frac{3}{4}$ inches high.

62 A pair of Bow figures, showing typical bases and applied leaves. Anchor-and-dagger mark. 8 inches high. *c.* 1760.

63 Three typical Bow figures with touches of underglaze-blue. The form of base and of the applied leaves are typical and worthy of note. Anchor-and-dagger marks. Centre figure 8 inches high. *c.* 1760.

Bristol

(c. 1749–52   soft-paste
c. 1770–81   hard-paste)

Bristol porcelain falls into two distinct groups. Firstly, we have that rare class made by Benjamin Lund and William Miller at Redcliff Backs, Bristol, during the period c. 1749–52. This class is soft-paste porcelain containing soap rock. The pieces normally show a strong Chinese influence. Apart from some very rare examples which display a moulded 'Bristol' or 'Bristoll' mark (see the *Illustrated Encyclopaedia of British Pottery and Porcelain*, Plates 79–80), the pieces do not bear a factory-mark and are very easily confused with the early Worcester porcelains. The Worcester management in fact took over the first Bristol concern early in 1752, and many pieces formerly attributed to Lund & Miller's Bristol factory now appear to be of Worcester manufacture.[1]

In 1770 a second porcelain factory was established at Bristol, by William Cookworthy. The basic body is true, or hard-paste, often showing wreathing and tears in the body of hand-thrown objects—such as bowls or cups—and in these respects the wares are similar to those from the other West Country factory at Plymouth, of which the Bristol concern was an offshoot. In 1774 the Bristol factory was continued by Richard Champion (& Co.) who continued to manufacture hard-paste porcelain until at least 1778. In 1780 Champion tried to sell his patent rights (for the manufacture of hard-paste porcelain) to Wedgwood, who, however, seems to have recommended other Staffordshire 'enterprising' potters who might have been interested in the patent. In fact the rights were sold to a group of Staffordshire potters who were to form what is now commonly known as the New Hall Company. The exact date of closure is open to doubt.

The Bristol porcelains of the 1770–78 period are quite rare. Most pieces found today comprise parts of tea services, and these range from simple, rather cottage floral designs to fine pieces in the Sèvres style. Several special sets were made incorporating the initials, crest, or arms of the purchaser (Plates 68–69). The flower-painting on Bristol porcelain can be most attractive. Attractive figures were made, also—though these are rarer—vases and the oval, often unglazed plaques. The latter were encrusted with superbly modelled flowers (Plate 74). The under-glaze-blue painted wares in general bear Chinese-styled designs (Plates 64–65).

[1] The results of recent excavations on the Worcester factory-site are discussed in Henry Sandon's *Illustrated Guide to Worcester Porcelain* (Barrie & Jenkins, London, 1969).

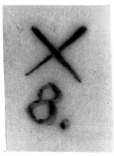

Much Bristol porcelain is unmarked, a cross in blue accompanied by a painter's or gilder's number can be regarded as the standard mark, and a copy of the Dresden crossed swords occurs, also with a number, see below. Some of the rare figures may bear the 'To' mark which is to be found on Bow, Caughley, and Worcester wares.

A good selection of Bristol porcelain is illustrated in F. Severne Mackenna's *Champion's Bristol Porcelain* (F. Lewis Ltd, Leigh-on-Sea, 1947). The same author's *Cookworthy's Plymouth and Bristol Porcelain* (F. Lewis Ltd, Leigh-on-Sea, 1946) is also of interest. The reader is warned that fake Bristol porcelain (often bearing the cross mark with a date) exists.

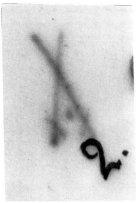

64 A Bristol hard-paste porcelain teapot painted in underglaze-blue with a Chinese-style design. Blue cross mark. 7 inches high. *c.* 1770–72.

65 A rare, blue-printed Bristol hard-paste plate and a blue-painted sauce-boat—the latter with cross mark. Diameter of plate $8\frac{1}{8}$ inches. *c.* 1770–74.

66 Two charming and typical
examples of Bristol hard-paste
porcelain, both having the
cross mark. Tea caddy and
cover 4 inches high. *c.* 1775.

67 A rare set of Bristol hard-paste figures of the elements: Fire, Air, Water, and Earth. Impressed 'To' mark. 10 to 11 inches high. *c.* 1775–78.

68 A selection of the rarer types of Bristol hard-paste porcelains but showing characteristic forms. *c.* 1775–78.

69 A simple but attractive Bristol tea bowl and saucer. The enamelled festoons of flowers represent a typical form of decoration. Blue enamel cross mark.

70 A moulded Bristol sugar-bowl and cover from a tea set, showing an attractive restraint of decoration. Underglaze-blue crossed-swords mark with blue enamel cross and number 7 in gold. 4¾ inches high. *c.* 1775.

71 A selection of typical Bristol hard-paste porcelain tea wares bearing the characteristic green-festoon design. *c.* 1770–78.

72 Bristol hard-paste porcelain tea wares, showing the Continental influence. *c.* 1775–78.

73 Some rare enamelled decoration on Bristol hard-paste porcelain, but the forms, especially of the handles, are noteworthy. *c.* 1770–78.

opposite page
74 A rare eighteenth-century Bristol hard-paste 'biscuit' (unglazed) porcelain plaque, the surround encrusted with superbly modelled flowers. This factory specialised in such small presentation plaques, but they are rarely found today. Large examples are of nineteenth-century date. $4\frac{1}{2} \times 3\frac{1}{2}$ inches.

75 A superb Bristol hard-paste porcelain covered urn or 'pot-pourri', richly gilt and encrusted with 'biscuit' flowers. $9\frac{1}{4}$ inches high. *c.* 1775.

Caughley

THOMAS TURNER'S 'SALOPIAN' PORCELAIN
(*c.* 1775–99)

Thomas Turner, who had been trained at the Worcester factory, moved northwards into Shropshire in about 1772 to convert an existing pottery into a porcelain manufactory at Caughley, some two miles south of Broseley. The factory was in open country, not on the bank of the River Severn but some two miles to the west of it. The detail from a contemporary estate-map shows the open plan of the factory with its three kilns, which were fired by coal mined on the other side of the narrow road, only a hundred yards away. The new Caughley factory was in production in 1775, when newspaper reports featured the new wares 'which in colour and fineness are truly elegant and beautiful and have the bright and lovely white of the so

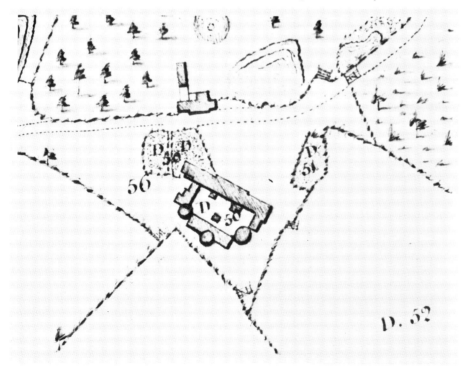

much extolled Oriental'. Much of the Caughley or 'Salopian' wares were painted or printed in underglaze-blue, with patterns showing pronounced Chinese influence.

Since the publication of my *Illustrated Encyclopaedia of British Pottery and Porcelain* in 1966, much new information has come to light as a result of finds on the factory-site, and a class of wares formerly believed to be Caughley has been shown to be Worcester. Briefly, the porcelains bearing printed mock-Chinese numeral-marks are Worcester, as are those examples bearing a printed crescent mark. Full details of the finds leading to this reclassification are given in my *Caughley and Worcester Porcelains, 1775–1800* (Herbert Jenkins, London, 1969). The basic true Caughley marks are the impressed word 'Salopian', the initial S (or 'Sx' or 'So') painted or printed in underglaze-blue, the initial C, and the hand-painted open crescent, but many examples are unmarked.

In the main, the Caughley porcelains appear very similar to those from Worcester, and the glaze-free line inside the foot-rim is a characteristic of both factories. The Caughley potting is rather thicker than the Worcester. The body by transmitted light has normally an orange tint rather than the green of Worcester, although both were of the soapstone type, showing on analysis a relatively high percentage of magnesia, over 10%. While several popular patterns were produced at both factories, those shown in Plates 80, 82, 84, and 90 were restricted to Caughley, and in other cases tell-tale differences in the shape or the added pattern point to the true origin. These differences are clearly shown in the specialist references and related articles listed at the end of this section.

While some 75% of the Caughley porcelains were decorated in underglaze-blue, some finely gilt and some enamelled pieces are to be found. Contemporary accounts and letters show that Thomas Turner sent large quantities of his 'Salopian' porcelain to be gilt and enamelled at the Chamberlain establishment at Worcester (page 100) and the teapot shown in Colour Plate II is a good example of this Chamberlain-decorated Caughley porcelain.

In general, Thomas Turner specialised in the manufacture of table wares, tea services, dessert sets, and (rarely) dinner services, and most pieces found today were once parts of such sets. Decorated with stock designs, such objects are still quite plentiful and are amongst the least expensive of the eighteenth-century porcelains. The rare pieces—sandwich-dishes, artichoke-cups, butter-tureens, chestnut-baskets, candlesticks, caudle-cups, custard-cups, egg-cups, eye-baths, finger-bowls, inkstands, mustard-pots, and the charming miniature pieces (Plates 90–91)—are justly more expensive, and some objects such as studs and buttons are known only by unfinished examples found on the factory-site. Some vases were made, but apparently not figures. The factory was taken over (and continued) by the Coalport management in 1799 (see page 149).

For a full review of the Caughley factory and its products, the reader is referred to *Caughley and Worcester Porcelains 1775–1800* by G. A. Godden (Herbert Jenkins, London, 1969). Magazine articles on facets of the same subject are: 'Caughley or Salopian Porcelain', *Collectors' Guide*, October 1967; 'Some Second Thoughts on Caughley', *Collectors' Guide*, August 1968; 'Worcester Blue-Printed Porcelains', *The Burlington Magazine*, January 1969; 'Some Unexpected Finds at Caughley', *The Connoisseur*, May 1969; 'Caughley Porcelain in the French Style', *Collectors' Guide: World of Antiques*, October 1968.

A very good representative display of Caughley porcelain can be seen at the Victoria and Albert Museum, London. The Clive House Museum at Shrewsbury also contains a good selection, including many pieces on loan from the Cronk and Godden collections.

76 A selection of Caughley cabbage-leaf jugs with mask-head spouts, showing typical underglaze-blue designs. The small jug depicts the iron bridge upstream from the factory. Note the rather narrow, lemon-like body, contrasting with the more rotund, orange-like body of the Worcester jugs of the same basic shape. Parrot jug, top left 8¾ inches high. 'Sx' mark. *c.* 1775–90. The jugs occur in various sizes and with different blue or enamelled designs.

77 A 'pull' from the original
engraving of the popular
Fisherman print. Note the 'S'
marks, top right.

78 A rare Caughley blue-
printed presentation jug with
two matching mugs. Jug 7¼
inches high 'S' marks. *c.* 1780.

80 A Caughley porcelain teapot of characteristic shape bearing the 'Nankin Willow' printed design, copied from a hand-painted Chinese original. Gilt border and enrichments. $5\frac{1}{2}$ inches high. 'S' printed mark. *c.* 1785.

81 A Caughley bowl bearing the 'Temple' print (Plate 79), showing the reverse side. Diameter $7\frac{1}{4}$ inches. 'S' printed mark. *c.* 1780–85.

opposite page
79 A fine Caughley coffee pot bearing the blue-printed 'Temple' pattern, a subject which also occurs, though rarely, on Worcester tea wares. $10\frac{1}{4}$ inches high. 'Sx' printed mark. *c.* 1780–85.

82 A rare Caughley radish dish bearing the blue, 'Full Nankin' print. Shown with an unglazed fragment from the factory-site. 11¼ inches long. *c.* 1785.

83 A Caughley teapot bearing a rare Chinese-style underglaze-blue print. 4¾ inches high. *c.* 1780–85.

84 A Caughley creamer of
unusual form bearing the blue,
'Fence and House' print—one
only found on Caughley
porcelains. 5 inches high.
c. 1785.

85 A rare Caughley covered
sauce-tureen bearing the
standard 'Full Nankin'
underglaze-blue print, widely
used on dessert, and dinner,
service pieces. $4\frac{1}{2}$ inches high.
c. 1785.

86 A Caughley blue-printed sauce-boat of a characteristic form. 5¾ inches long—each standard shape was made in several different sizes. *c.* 1780–85.

87 A Caughley sauce-boat decorated with a French-style underglaze-blue sprig design. Shown with a fragment of the original plaster mould. 8 inches long. *c.* 1785–90.

88 A Caughley eye-bath bearing the blue Fisherman print and an unglazed 'waster' from the factory-site. $1\frac{9}{10}$ inches high. *c.* 1785–90.

89 Two Caughley egg-strainers bearing the Fisherman print and an asparagus-server (not a knife-rest as they are sometimes called). Many fragments of such pieces were found on the factory-site and they are mentioned in contemporary accounts. Drainers $3\frac{1}{10}$ inches in diameter. *c.* 1785–90.

90 A blue-painted dish from a miniature (toy) Caughley dinner service shown with 'wasters' from the factory-site, including —bottom left—a painted but unglazed plate complete with the 'S' mark. This plate is only an inch in diameter. *c.* 1785–90.

91 Representative pieces from a Caughley miniature or toy tea and coffee service bearing the popular Fisherman print. The 'S' mark can be seen on the upturned tea bowl. Coffee pot 3¾ inches high. *c.* 1785–90.

Colour Plate II A superb Caughley porcelain teapot, the top borders decorated in underglaze-blue. It is probable that this pot, then bearing only the blue borders, was sent to Chamberlain's decorating establishment at Worcester where the gilt ornamentation and crest were added to fulfil a special order. Several similar Worcester-decorated Caughley wares are featured in *Caughley and Worcester Porcelains, 1775–1800* by G. A. Godden (Herbert Jenkins, London, 1969). 'S' mark in underglaze-blue. $5\frac{3}{4}$ inches high. *c.* 1790.

92 A selection of 'S'-marked
Caughley porcelains decorated
with French-style sprig
patterns in underglaze-blue.
Such designs were popular in
the 1790s, and at this period
several Continental shapes were
directly copied at the Caughley
factory. Jug $9\frac{1}{4}$ inches high.

93 A fine and rare Caughley dessert dish, the centre painted in underglaze-blue, with gilt surround. Impressed 'Salopian' mark. 12¼ inches long. *c.* 1790.

94 Caughley porcelains bearing the underglaze-blue 'Royal Lily' pattern, a design more often found on Worcester porcelains. Note the standard 'S' mark on the upturned bowl. Egg cup 1¾ inches high. *c.* 1790.

95 A gilt Caughley tea set, showing representative shapes of the 1785–95 period. Such forms were decorated in very many styles both in underglaze-blue and in enamels. Teapot $5\frac{3}{4}$ inches high. *c.* 1790.

Chamberlain-Worcester

ROBERT CHAMBERLAIN, CHAMBERLAIN & CO., ETC.
(*c.* 1788–1852)

This section follows naturally from that relating to the Caughley factory, for after Robert Chamberlain had broken his connection with the main Worcester factory in about 1788 he purchased white porcelain from Thomas Turner at Caughley (page 85) and added decoration in his own studio, helped by former Worcester enamellers and gilders. Some of this Caughley porcelain was decorated for Thomas Turner and sent back to Caughley or to Turner's London warehouse, but some was decorated for Chamberlain's account and sold in his own retail shop in High Street, Worcester.

The two cabbage-leaf jugs shown in Plate 96 are of Caughley make, but their decoration and sale are recorded in Chamberlain's 1790 account-book which is included in this illustration. Many of the original Chamberlain factory-records have been preserved and have added greatly to our knowledge of the Chamberlain products. The plate shown in Plate 97 left the Caughley factory only with the underglaze-blue border and mark added. After being painted in over-glaze enamels at the Chamberlain decorating establishment, the mark was covered by a gilt blob, indicating that it was a piece sold by Chamberlain, not an example for the Caughley account. Other examples of Chamberlain-decorated Caughley porcelain are featured in my *Caughley and Worcester Porcelains 1775–1800* (Herbert Jenkins, London, 1969) and the teapot shown in Colour Plate II shows well the quality of the early Chamberlain decoration on Caughley porcelains.

The dependence on the supply of Caughley porcelain presented many difficulties, and by 1791 the Chamberlains—that is, Robert and his son Humphrey—were producing their own porcelain, although for some few years the supply was extremely limited and they continued to purchase some from Turner of Caughley. The initial difficulties had been overcome by 1796 when Royal services were being made, and figures and ornate centrepieces were included in the products.

In general, however, the Chamberlain-Worcester porcelains of the 1790s comprised tea services painted with rather simple but attractive designs (Plates 98 and 99). This is not to say that sumptuous wares were not made. They were—especially fine vases and tumblers, painted with figure-subject panels in the style of the Flight-Worcester porcelains (page 431). Some of this fine figure-painting was the work of Humphrey Chamberlain, and the best bird-painting, such as that shown in Plate 100, was the work of George Davis. Many fine pieces were also painted with shell or feather panels. In 1802 Lord Nelson visited the works and placed an order for several services. The teapot shown in Plate 108 is from one such Nelson set and illustrates well the quality of the Worcester work and the contemporary taste for the gay, colourful, so-called 'Japan' patterns. In contrast, some attractive pieces were made in the unglazed 'biscuit' porcelain (Plate 110). Some very attractive glazed and 'biscuit' animal models were also made (see Plate 111).

In 1840 the two former rival firms of Flight, Barr & Barr and Chamberlains were amalgamated, but without the old rivalry the new firm of Chamberlain & Co. lost much of its prestige. The porcelains made between 1840 and 1852 are rather heavy and badly designed (to modern eyes), but the old quality can be seen especially in some painted trays, the borders of which are enriched with relief-modelled flowers or shells. A popular innovation of the 1840s was the pierced wares (Plate 115). The engraving right shows a typical piece of this type. It appeared in the *Art Union* magazine of March 1846. In 1852 the new Kerr & Binns partnership (page 417) succeeded Chamberlains, and in 1862 this gave way to the Royal Worcester Company which continues to this day. (See page 417.)

The early Chamberlain porcelains of the 1791–93 period appear to have been unmarked. Later one finds various painted marks applied to the inside of teapot and sugar-basin covers, reading, for example, 'Chamberlains, Worcester' with the pattern-number added; but other pieces in the tea set bore only the pattern-number, which was always in simple (non-fractional) form. In the nineteenth century several painted or printed marks were employed, and these can normally be dated to narrow limits by reference to the changes listed below:

From 1807 words relating to the patronage of the Prince of Wales may be included.

From 1811 the word 'Royal' may appear, also a crown device. The description 'Regent China' also occurs from this period on pieces made from a special hard-looking, expensive body.

From the later part of 1813 the address of the London shop, at 63 Piccadilly, was incorporated in most marks until May 1816.

From July 1816 the address of the new shop at 155 New Bond Street appears, and from 1840 a further address, 1 Coventry Street, was added. Some rare pieces will be found bearing both a Flight, Barr & Barr mark—normally the initials F. B. B. impressed—as well as a Chamberlain mark. Such double-marked pieces relate to the amalgamation of the two concerns, the old F.B.B. pieces being decorated and sold by the new 'Chamberlain & Co.' concern.

The full story of the Chamberlain products, supported by a mass of contemporary documents, is given in my specialist book *Chamberlain-Worcester Porcelain 1788–1852* Barrie & Jenkins, 1982). This work will be found to include the key Chamberlain shapes, by which means the mostly unmarked porcelains can be identified.

The Chamberlain pattern-numbers progress in simple sequence.

96 A pair of Caughley porcelain cabbage-leaf jugs which were sent in the 'white' to Chamberlain of Worcester. These jugs were supplied in March 1790 to a Mr James Kindon of Birmingham, as is evidenced by the original account-book entry:

'2 Quart jugs, gold edge and line, with cypher crest and shield @ 15/- £1.10.0.'

Chamberlains decorated much Caughley porcelain before they started to manufacture their own wares.

97 An 'S'-marked Caughley
plate with underglaze-blue
border. The enamelled centre
and gilt borders were added at
Chamberlain's decorating
establishment. The gilding is
very fine, but the painting,
especially of the horses, is
somewhat wooden and not up
to the standard of the main
Worcester factory. Diameter
6¾ inches. *c.* 1790.

opposite page
98 A typical early Chamberlain fluted or 'shanked' tea set. The same basic shapes appear also plain without fluting—the sprigs are in brown and gold. This is pattern 21. Marked inside covers 'Chamberlain. Worcester. Warranted, 21.' Teapot 6 inches high. *c.* 1795.

99 A further selection of early Worcester tea-ware forms painted with pattern 34. These shapes can also occur in the unfluted version. Marked inside covers, 'Chamberlains. Worc. Warranted. 34.' Teapot 7 inches high. *c.* 1795–1800.

101 A fine pair of
Chamberlain-Worcester jugs of
a characteristic, standard shape,
the panels painted with views
of Cambridge and of Worcester.
Borders and alternate flutes
painted in underglaze-blue.
6¾ inches high. *c.* 1800–1805.

opposite page
100 A superb Chamberlain dish
from a dessert service, the
centre by George Davis, a
famous Worcester bird-painter.
Similar painting was earlier
applied to Caughley blanks.
Gilt mark 'Chamberlains
Worcester'. 8½ × 7¼ inches.
c. 1795–1800.

107

opposite page
104 Representative pieces from a Chamberlain-Worcester dessert service enamelled with the popular 'Bishop Sumner' design, a pattern favoured at several other factories— including the rival Worcester firm—at all periods from about 1765 onwards. In the Chamberlain records this is entered as pattern 75, and such pieces should bear this identifying number. Marked 'Chamberlains Worcester No. 75'. Centrepiece 12 inches long. *c.* 1800.

102 A typical early Chamberlain coffee pot painted in underglaze-blue and gold. Marked 'Chamberlains Worcester, No. 31'. 9¾ inches high. *c.* 1795.

03 Two typical Chamberlain umblers, finely painted, with igure-subjects in the taste of he period. Very similar styles vere also favoured at the rival light-Worcester factory. These ubjects appear listed in the Chamberlain account-books n 1798 and 1799. Marked in gold 'Chamberlains. Worcester'. 1¼ and 3⅜ inches high. *c.* 1798–800.

105 An apricot-ground
Chamberlain vase of fine
quality. 'Chamberlain Worcester'
written mark. 5¼ inches high.
c. 1805.

106 A Chamberlain pot-pourri
vase of typical form. '
'Chamberlain Worcester'
written mark. 7¼ inches high.
c. 1810.

opposite page
107 An important
Chamberlain-Worcester vase,
finely painted with landscape-
panel. The gilding on the neck
is of a typical Worcester type.
'Chamberlain's Worcester'
written mark. 14¼ inches high.
c. 1810–15.

108 A richly decorated teapot from the service ordered by Admiral Lord Nelson in 1802, showing the high standards reached by this factory at this period. Written name-mark inside cover.

109 A dessert dish of characteristic shape, but with the rare feature of openwork edges. Written mark 'Chamberlains Worcester. Manufacturers to their Royal Highnesses the Prince of Wales and Duke of Cumberland.' $9\frac{1}{2} \times 7\frac{1}{4}$ inches. *c.* 1810.

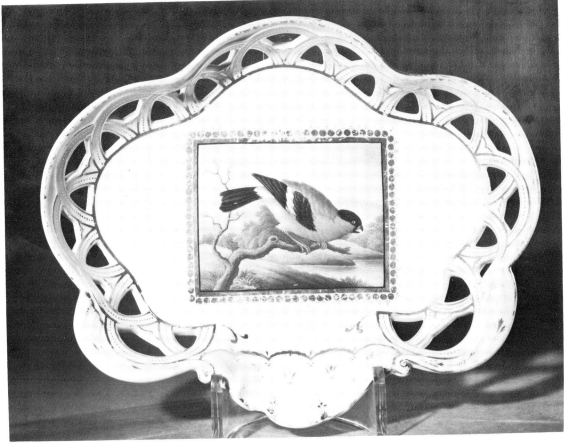

110 A rare Chamberlain-Worcester portrait-bust of the Duke of York, in biscuit (unglazed) porcelain. Incised mark 'H Chamberlain & Sons. Manufacturers to his Majesty. Worcester & 155 Bond St. London.' $9\frac{1}{2}$ inches high. *c.* 1820.

111 A selection of
Chamberlain-Worcester animal
models. These are normally
posed on a matt, dark-blue
base and have written
'Chamberlains Worcester'
marks. Rabbit 2¼ inches high.
c. 1815–25.

112 A typical blue-ground Chamberlain-Worcester vase of the basic Empire shape favoured by most English and Continental firms of the 1815–1830 period. This example shows the fine-quality flower-painting to be found on much Worcester porcelain. Written 'Chamberlain Worcester' mark. One of a set of three. $8\frac{1}{2}$ inches high. *c.* 1820–25.

opposite page

113 A rare shell-encrusted inkstand. These desk sets were popular at all factories. Written Chamberlain name-mark. 11 inches long. *c.* 1840.

114 A fine and typical Chamberlain-Worcester tray with shell-encrusted edge. The centre painted, in a typical stippled style, with a view of Bournemouth. Written 'Chamberlains Worcester' mark. 13¼ inches long. *c.* 1840–45.

115 Two typical examples of Chamberlain's reticulated porcelains of the 1840s, copied from Sèvres prototypes. These wares were featured in the *Illustrated London News* of 17 February 1849, but later porcelains in this general style were made by the Royal Worcester Company and by the Grainger-Worcester firm (see page 257). Jug 4¾ inches high. Written 'Chamberlain & Co. Worcester' marks. *c.* 1850.

Chelsea

CHELSEA
(*c.* 1745–69)

Of all the eighteenth-century English porcelain, that made at Chelsea in London is the most widely known and often the most expensive, two factors which have given rise to numerous reproductions.

Chelsea porcelain is of the soft-paste variety, the glaze is soft and has a friendly, waxy feel. Prior to about 1755 the glaze was whitened with oxide of tin, giving it a cream-like appearance.

The various periods of Chelsea porcelain are generally classified according to the anchor-like mark, but two other marks occur on the earliest pieces. The incised triangle mark (Plate 118) often occurs on the 'Goat and Bee' moulded jugs (Plate H) with the date 1745. A mark comprising a trident piercing a crown, painted in underglaze-blue, also occurs, on a rare class of Chelsea porcelain of the 1745–47 period.

Turning to the anchor marks, we find this device first appearing moulded in relief on an oval, raised pad (Plate 120), giving rise to the term 'raised-anchor' (*c.* 1749–52). Sometimes the anchor motif is picked out in red enamel, but mostly the mark is white. The porcelains of this period have the tin-added glaze and are modestly decorated with Oriental or simple, floral designs (Plate 123). Some of the early figure models are completely undecorated. The Chelsea figures and groups are slip-cast rather than press-moulded. (See pages 17–19.)

Some of the dish and plate shapes, as well as some of the jugs and sauce-boats, are modelled on silver designs, a fact that is not surprising when we recall that Nicholas Sprimont (1716–71), the factory manager for most of the period, was originally a Huguenot silversmith.

The next period is that known as the 'red-anchor' period (*c.* 1752–56) when the anchor was painted directly on to the porcelain in this colour. It should be noted that the anchor was neatly painted and that it was of small size, less than a quarter of an inch in height, although the size tended to increase in the 1760s. On figures and groups the anchor was often almost hidden away, and only on reproductions is it prominent.

Colour Plate III, with Plate 124 showing the reverse of the same dish, illustrates well the character of the red-anchor Chelsea porcelains. The enamel decoration is sparse. Moths, insects, or leaves are arranged so as to cover slight faults such as specks or bubbles in the glaze. A simple line-border runs round the edge. Turning to the underside, the foot-rim has had to be ground level, slight tears or other faults are to be seen in the body, and if one holds the object to the light, small pinpricks or 'moons' will show up (Plate 119). These are due to air bubbles within the body. Plates, dishes, and saucers were normally supported in the glost-kiln on small stilts, resulting in three or four 'stilt-marks' being left under the finished article. In general, these Chelsea porcelains are rather thickly potted and heavy to hold, although in over-all effect and despite all the above-mentioned minor blemishes, they are probably the most attractive of any English porcelain.

While there is no separate 'brown-anchor' period, it must be stated that the anchor device quite often appears painted in this colour on wares of the so-called red-anchor period and even into the 1760s. This was probably nothing more than a matter of convenience, as the brush (termed a 'pencil' in the ceramic industry) was ready charged with this pigment, the liner having painted the border in this colour as the last decorating operation. It will be observed that the brown anchor normally only appears on flat-wares having the brown line-edge (Plates 129, 130, 136–37), it is not found on figures and groups.

The charm of the red-anchor figures is readily seen in Plates 131 and 133. The latter especially shows the pleasing restraint of the decoration, even though no photograph can do justice to the warm, soft glaze. Note also the simple bases and the lack of floral bocage.

In the succeeding 'gold-anchor' period, that is, approximately 1756–69, during which time the anchor was painted in gold, the general designs became more florid and rococo, with use being made of a rich, streaky underglaze-blue, which was rather prone to bleed or run, necessitating the use of ornate, gilt borders to mask the uneven panel edges. For this characteristic see Plate 138, the top edge. The vases shown in Plate 140 are good and typical examples of the gold-anchor taste and show the rather lavish use of gold. This old honey-gilding is superb, often being slightly raised, with the petals of a flower or the veins of a leaf being 'tooled' or incised.

The gold-anchor figures were mounted on scroll bases; supporting floral bocages were often employed (Plate 144), although they were not so popular at Chelsea as at Bow, the colouring is more flamboyant than on the earlier figures. It is the gold-anchor-period figures that were so often copied, and Plate 145 illustrates three such reproductions made by Samson of Paris approximately a hundred years ago. Many later forgers have flooded the market with inferior work so that now even the Samson reproductions are becoming 'collectors' pieces' in their own right. I have used the description 'forgers' because these late Continental objects invariably bear the Chelsea gold-anchor mark, nearly always quite prominently placed and of a larger size (compare Plate 124 with Plate 125).

In contrast to the often large gold-anchor-period Chelsea figures and vases, there is a class of Chelsea 'toys', often only an inch or so in height. These toys, which took the form of seals (Plate 134), or scent bottles (Plate 135), or toothpick cases, were often mounted in gold or pinchbeck and were apparently sold by jewellers. The range of such pieces is huge, and the standard work on this facet of the Chelsea products is still G. E. Bryant's *Chelsea Porcelain Toys* which was published by the Medici Society, London, in 1925.

The gold-anchor-period Chelsea porcelains have a percentage of bone ash in the composition, resulting in a somewhat open, light body—in comparison with the earlier porcelain, which was of the glassy type. The glaze tended to be rather thickly applied and crazing (a network of fine lines) will often be seen in the glaze covering the gold-anchor wares.

Whilst we have been mainly concerned in this brief outline with the differing periods called after the standard marks, it must be understood that many pieces do not bear any mark and their attribution depends on the study of the characteristics as shown by the marked pieces (see, for example, Plate 124). There was also some overlap of marks employed, so that it is reasonable to assume that an ungilded piece made early in the gold-anchor period may have been given a red- or brown-anchor mark. The various periods are not therefore to be regarded as watertight compartments, but merely as general guides.

It should be borne in mind that the eighteenth-century Chelsea porcelains do not bear a pattern-number, except for some few two- or three-piece items such as a tureen, cover, and stand, which may have numbers painted under the anchor, relating each article to its proper companion. With the exception of the few early pieces which bear the incised Chelsea name-mark, no object bearing a mark incorporating the word 'Chelsea' will directly relate to the original factory, but they will be late nineteenth- or twentieth-century pieces which the manufacturers, rightly or wrongly, believe to be in the Chelsea style.

In August 1769 the Chelsea Porcelain Works were put up for sale by auction and the works and working materials were sold to James Cox. He, in turn, sold them to William Duesbury of the Derby factory in February 1770. The following so-called Chelsea-Derby wares of the 1770–84 period are discussed and illustrated separately in the next section.

The separate class of 'Girl in a Swing' porcelains is discussed on page 240.

Most general reference-books illustrate a selection of Chelsea porcelains, including my *Illustrated Encyclopaedia of British Pottery and Porcelain* (Herbert Jenkins, London, 1966)[1]. Specialist books are: *Chelsea Porcelain, the Triangle and Raised Anchor Wares* (1948), *Chelsea Porcelain, the Red Anchor Wares* (1951), *Chelsea Porcelain, the Gold Anchor Period* (1952), each by F. S. Mackenna, published by F. Lewis, Leigh-on-Sea. To which one should add *English Porcelain Figures of the 18th Century* by A. Lane (Faber & Faber, London, 1961) and *English Porcelain, 1745– 1850*, edited by R. J. Charleston (E. Benn, London, 1965), Chelsea section by J. V. G. Mallet. A good modern work is Elizabeth Adams' *Chelsea Porcelain* (Barrie & Jenkins, London, 1987).

---

[1] It should be said that the white shell-shaped sauce-boat shown in Plate 119 of that book is now believed to be Derby rather than Chelsea.

Colour Plate III A typical Chelsea dish of the early 1750s, with a rather thick white glaze slightly spotted and crazed. The enamelled line-edge and scattered flower-sprays with insects are quite typical of the period. The seemingly haphazard arrangement of the insects and sprays was in fact positioned to mask faults in the glaze—witness the leaf to the left of the moth. Diameter $9\frac{1}{4}$ inches. Plate 124, shows the reverse side with the small-sized red-anchor mark.
c. 1752–56.

116 An early Chelsea teacup decorated in the Oriental style, turned to show the rare trident mark in underglaze-blue. $2\frac{7}{8}$ inches high. *c.* 1745–7.

117 A very rare, early Chelsea, white porcelain group formed by the slip-cast method of moulding (see page 19) and marked with the blue trident-mark (see above). $3\frac{3}{4}$ inches high. *c.* 1745–47.

118 The underside of an early Chelsea oval, shell-shaped salt-cellar, showing the incised triangle-mark which should be under the glaze, not cut through it. *c.* 1745.

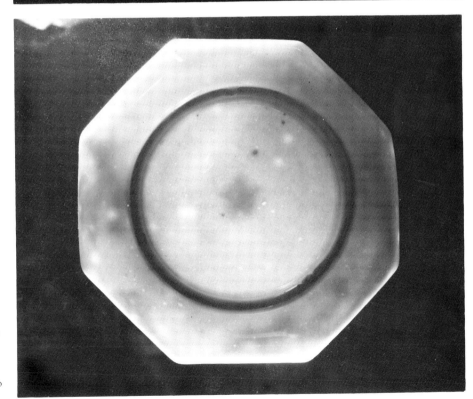

119 The reverse of an early Chelsea saucer of typical shape, photographed against the light to show the characteristic 'moons' and pinpricks caused by air holes in the body. Longton Hall porcelain can also show these faults.

120 The rear of a Chelsea white figure, showing the 'raised-anchor' mark arrowed. The anchor on enamelled specimens can be picked out in red. *c.* 1749–52.

121 A red-anchor-marked Chelsea plate enamelled in the Japanese style. The scene shows a man about to break a vase in which a child is stuck. Diameter 9½ inches. *c.* 1752–1755.

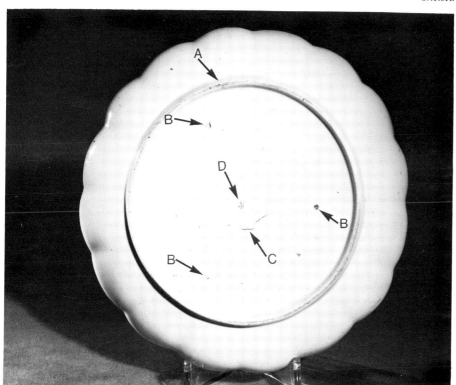

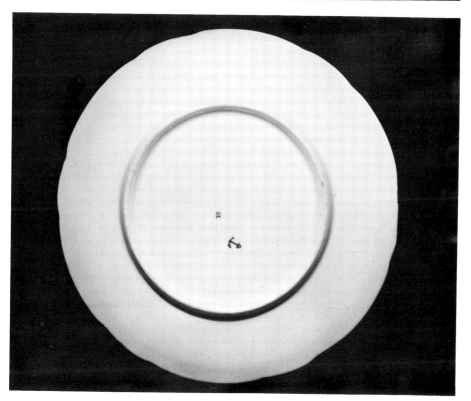

opposite page
122 A typical early Chelsea creamer and tea bowl, painted with Fable subjects by a hand well known on Chelsea porcelains of the 1750–55 period. The shapes and general style of decoration are noteworthy. Creamer 3½ inches high. *c.* 1752–55.

123 A fine and rare raised-anchor-marked Chelsea porcelain bowl, painted in the Japanese Kakiemon style. Diameter 6¼ inches. *c.* 1750.

124 The reverse of the dish shown in Colour Plate III, illustrating (a) the ground foot-rim, (b) the three stilt-marks on which it was supported in the kiln, (c) the faults in the body, and (d) the small size of the red-anchor mark.

125 The reverse of a French hard-paste reproduction-Chelsea plate of the 1900 period. Note the clean, unblemished appearance, the true foot-rim, and the relatively large-sized anchor mark.

126 A rare Chelsea covered box in pineapple form. The 1755 auction sale of Chelsea wares featured 'Two fine pineapples for desart'. Red-anchor marked. 7 inches high. *c.* 1755.

127 A fine, covered box in the form of a bunch of asparagus. Such items were mentioned in the 1756 sale-catalogue, and by this period the former white, almost opaque, glaze had been replaced by a more translucent, glassy glaze. Red-anchor mark. 7 inches long. *c.* 1756.

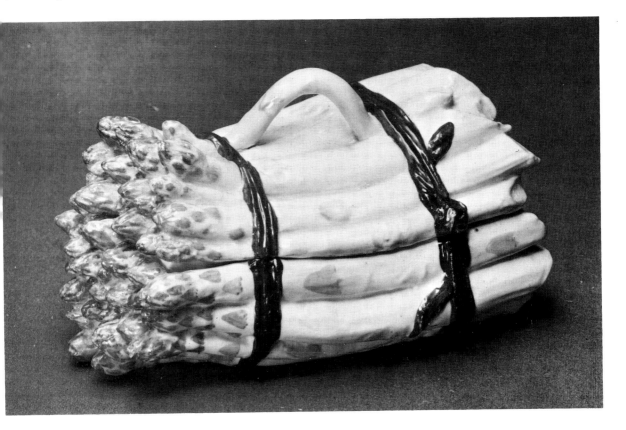

128 A superb red-anchor-
marked Chelsea dish with
relief-moulded border design,
the enamelled Fable panels in
the style of O'Neale. 11½ inches
long. *c.* 1752–55.

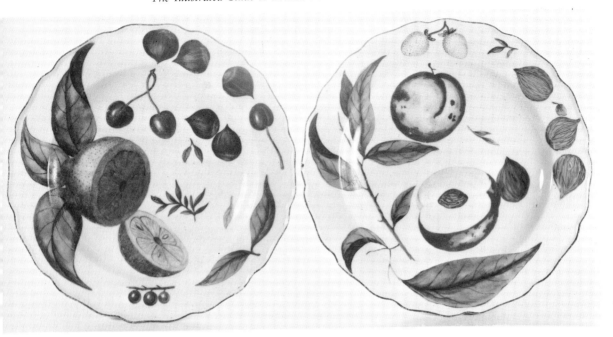

129 A pair of Chelsea dessert plates, boldly painted in a characteristic style. Brown-anchor marks. Diameter 8¼ inches. *c.* 1755.

130 A fine Chelsea botanical plate, the design taken from *Plantae et Papiliones* by G. D. Ehret. Brown-anchor marks. Diameter 9⅛ inches. *c.* 1755.

131 A charming set of the Four Seasons in Chelsea porcelain of the red-anchor period. The figure of Winter is in this case the only one marked—illustrating the point that much Chelsea, and other eighteenth-century, porcelains do *not* bear a factory-mark. 5¼ inches high. *c.* 1755.

132 A typical example of Chelsea copying Italian Comedy figures, probably from a Continental porcelain prototype. Red-anchor marked. 5½ inches high. *c.* 1755.

opposite page
134 Four typical Chelsea porcelain seals, among many such 'toys' which were mounted by jewellers. Average height 1¼ inch. *c.* 1760.

135 A Miniature Chelsea seal and two typical scent-bottles, 3½ inches high. *c.* 1760–65.

133 A fine pair of Chelsea red-anchor-period figures representing Astronomy and Painting, showing with the Seasons, in Plate 131, the charming restraint of decoration and good modelling of this period. The warm, soft glaze is apparent even in the photographic reproduction. 5¼ × 5⅜ inches high. *c.* 1755.

136 A typical Chelsea dish, part of a set of eight dishes and twenty-two plates. Brown-anchor marks. 12¾ inches long. *c.* 1755.

137 A further Chelsea dessert dish painted in a typical style— one that is also found on reproductions. Brown-anchor mark. 10 × 7¼ inches. *c.* 1755.

138 A Chelsea handleless cup, the ground painted with a characteristic, deep, streaky blue. Figure-painting of this type is rare and valuable. Gold-anchor mark. 3¾ inches high. *c.* 1760–65.

139 Part of a gold-anchor-marked Chelsea tea set, the borders painted with the rare claret colour. The surfaces relief-moulded with a pine-cone-like design. Teapot 9 inches high. *c.* 1765–70.

133

140 A fine and typical pair of
gold-anchor-period Chelsea
vases with the rich blue ground.
Superb, tooled gilding and rare
figure-painting. 10 inches high.
c. 1765.

opposite page
141 A superb pair of
Chelsea porcelain vases having
very fine gilding and attractive
figure-painting. Gold-anchor
marks. 10¾ inches high. *c.* 1765.

143 Three lively Chelsea masquerade figures copied from a contemporary print by Bowles, after Maurer. Gold-anchor mark. 8¼ and 8 inches high. *c.* 1760.

opposite page
142 An ornate pair of Chelsea vases painted with a claret ground. The shapes, while perhaps not 'pure', are typical of the period. Gold-anchor marks. 12½ inches high. *c.* 1760–65.

144 An attractive Chelsea figure, the Imperial Shepherd, decorated in typical manner with gilt enrichment. Gold-anchor mark. 12¼ inches high. *c.* 1765.

145 Three seemingly typical Chelsea gold-anchor-period animal-candlestick groups but of hard-paste porcelain made by Samson of Paris in the nineteenth century. Samson's reproductions are of very fine quality. Gold-anchor mark. Centre group 12¼ inches high. *c.* 1860.

Chelsea-Derby

CHELSEA-DERBY
(1770–84)

This joint-name has been used by collectors to indicate the porcelains made at the Chelsea factory in London between 1770 and 1784—after this factory had been purchased by William Duesbury of the Derby porcelain factory. Figures and groups of the type shown in Plates 146–47 with 'pad-marks' under the bases (Plate 146) are traditionally termed 'Chelsea-Derby'. However, the attribution of porcelains to Chelsea in the 1770–84 period is difficult and little research has been carried out to clarify the position, the specialist books on each factory tending to disregard the transitional period.

The situation is complicated by the fact that a general exchange of moulds, working materials, and even workmen took place, and that, as contemporary records show, wares made at Chelsea often used 'Darby Clay', so that the porcelain body does not necessarily offer a guide to the place of origin.

In my opinion, the figures of the type shown in Plates 146–47 (and in Plate 151 of my *Illustrated Encyclopaedia of British Pottery and Porcelain*) are of Derby manufacture of the 1760–75 period and have no connection with Chelsea. The examples do not appear to have been made from known Chelsea moulds, although some are close copies of Chelsea examples. If they were, in fact, Chelsea-Derby, the Chelsea moulds would have been readily available for use. Also the general character and appearance are vastly different from the gold-anchor-marked Chelsea porcelains of the 1760s. The modelling is sharp and the glaze is thin, quite different from the rich thick glaze which tends to blunt the modelling on the gold-anchor-marked Chelsea figures.

The ornate, gold-anchor-marked perfume pot shown in Colour Plate IV is, however, a link between the Chelsea and Derby factories. The Chelsea model was represented in the March 1755 sale of Chelsea porcelains. The description of Lot 58 sold on the ninth day reads 'a large beautiful Perfume Pot chased and gilt, enamel'd with flowers, with a figure representing Meleager with a boar's head'. But this example is from the 1770s and the flower-painting is similar to that found on Derby useful wares. The problem is to know if the Chelsea moulds for this piece were sent to Derby where these former Chelsea models may have been reproduced, or whether this pot was made at Chelsea some fifteen or more years after its original introduction. My own view (unsupported by any evidence) is that this was made at Derby perhaps for sale at Duesbury's London showrooms, or at the London auction sales which featured Duesbury & Co.'s products.

Messrs Duesbury & Co.'s London showroom at 8 Bedford Street, Covent Garden, was opened in June 1773. A related trade-card in the Victoria and Albert Museum is reproduced below. The engraved articles show no relation to the so-called Chelsea-Derby figures of the type shown in Plates 146–47. The objects represented show the classical influence then favoured at Derby, and the fine 'biscuit' figures and groups, one of the specialities of the Derby factory, are particularly listed in this card of 'Duesbury & Co; Manufacturers of Derby & Chelsea Porcelain'.

Certain Derby or Chelsea-Derby wares are marked with a gold anchor as previously employed by the Chelsea factory. Plates 150 and A show both sides of a typical example. The plate has none of the characteristic blemishes of the early Chelsea examples (Plate 124) or even the ground-off foot found on typical gold-anchor-period Chelsea plates with their surplus of glaze. Again I believe that this and related wares such as those shown in Plates 151–52 were made at the Derby factory and that the gold-anchor mark was added to goods sold from the London shop (the continuation of the Chelsea anchor mark would add prestige). A gold-anchor-marked bowl in the Victoria and Albert Museum bears the date 1779 (Plate 148, *An Illustrated Encyclopaedia of British Pottery and Porcelain*) and gives proof that the Chelsea anchor mark was continued at Derby or at the taken-over Chelsea works until at least this date.

It should be noted that at this period—the 1770s—there was no regular Derby factory-mark although a device of a 'D' and an anchor, and also a crowned anchor, was introduced, in all probability to mark the union of the Chelsea and the Derby factories. The 'D'-and-anchor mark was certainly in use by 1773.

Excavations at the Chelsea factory-site have already shown that useful wares in the restrained style of the late 1770s were indeed produced there after Duesbury took over. 'Wasters' of tea wares rather like that shown in Plate 245 (a teapot bearing the Derby crowned 'D' mark in puce) were found at Chelsea, underlining the very real difficulty in distinguishing between the products of the two factories. Almost certainly the output at Chelsea between 1770 and 1784 was quite small, but it must be noted that the porcelains are well potted and most attractive.

140

Apart from the Chelsea accounts and letters quoted by Llewellynn Jewitt in his *Ceramic Art of Great Britain*, the catalogues of the sales held in London of Duesbury & Co.'s porcelains afford good evidence of the productions of the period. Unfortunately no indication of the place of manufacture is given, all lots being grouped under headings such as 'An elegant and extensive assortment of Derby and Chelsea Porcelain'. On 18 and 19 February 1778 there was held a sale of 'Part of the remaining stock of the Chelsea Porcelain Manufactory',[1] with 'the remainder of the valuable stock' being sold in May 1778. This would suggest that the Chelsea factory was not still in production, although we know from a letter quoted by Jewitt that the buildings remained until at least February 1784. 'We are pretty forward in the pulling down of the building at Chelsea. I think a little better than a fortnight they will be all down to the ground. . . .' (The letter is dated 18 February 1784.) Notwithstanding the two sales in 1778 of the remaining stock of the Chelsea factory, Duesbury's London sales continued to include Chelsea-type wares, perhaps unsold items or newly decorated remainders (such pieces are often sold as Chelsea on account of the gold-anchor marks which they bear). The important large pair of vases shown in Plate 153 are a case in point. Sold for £200 in 1967 as Chelsea, they were originally sold to Lady Paget (for eighteen guineas) in May 1781 and were described in Duesbury's sale as:

A pair of uncommonly large octagon jars (near 2 feet high) decorated with natural flowers and finely enamelled with figures, landscapes, &c, richly ornamented with chased and burnished gold, the figures representing a votaress of Bacchus and Innocence washing her hands at an altar.

Whether we call these Chelsea, Chelsea-Derby, or Derby, they are vastly different from the figures and groups which are traditionally called Chelsea-Derby (Plates 146–47).

As previously indicated, the Chelsea works were demolished early in 1784, and the remaining working materials were sold or transferred to Derby.

The Chelsea-Derby porcelains do not bear pattern-numbers.

---

[1] These sales, advertised as being the remaining stock of the Chelsea Porcelain Manufactory, obviously included Derby porcelain, for we find featured typical Derby wares such as 'Biscuit groups and single figures in abundance' (see page 216).

146 A pair of so-called Chelsea-Derby figures, which should more correctly be classed as Derby. Note the three 'pad-marks' under the upturned base. Unmarked. 8¾ inches high. *c.* 1760–65.

opposite page
147 A large and well-modelled 'Chelsea-Derby' *cum* Derby figure of Mars the modelling being sharper than contemporary Chelsea figures as the glaze was less inclined to fill the recesses. Pad-marks under base. 13½ inches high. *c.* 1765.

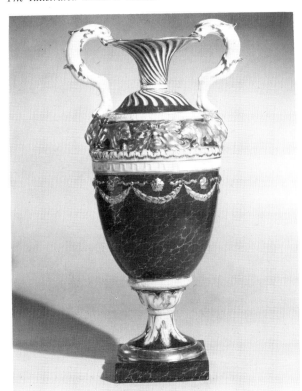

148 A tall blue-enamelled and gilt Chelsea-Derby vase, showing the new classical influence. 16¼ inches high. *c.* 1775.

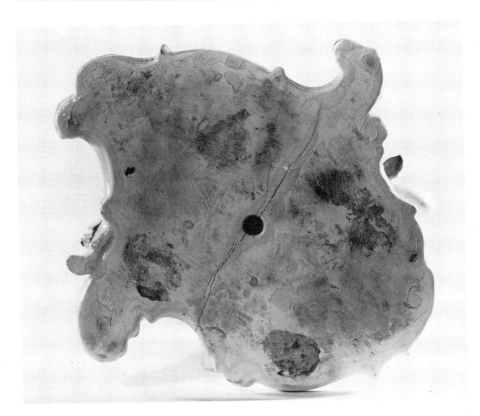

149 The base of the pot-pourri shown in Colour Plate IV, illustrating the Derby-type pad-marks (the darker blobs) and typical fire-cracks.

Colour Plate IV One of a pair of Chelsea-Derby type pot-pourri vases (pierced cover not shown), perhaps made at the Derby factory from original Chelsea moulds. This model was first included in the Chelsea sale of March 1755— 'A large beautiful Perfume Pot chased and gilt, enamell'd with flowers, with a figure representing Meleager with a boar's head.' Gold-anchor mark. $13\frac{1}{4}$ inches high. *c.* 1775–80.

150 & A An attractive Chelsea-Derby plate marked with the gold anchor. Turquoise and gilt border. The lower illustration shows the reverse side and the improvement in potting technique since the red-anchor period (compare with Plate 124). Diameter 9 inches. *c.* 1775–80.

151 A Chelsea-Derby teapot, showing rather more severe taste in comparison with the gold-anchor wares with their ground colours or ornate borders. 6 inches high. *c.* 1775–80.

opposite page
152 A superb pair of Chelsea-Derby ewers, illustrating well the new classical influence. These shapes were re-used at Derby at later periods and copied at other nineteenth-century factories. The Derby gilding at this period is somewhat prone to flaking—note the mask-head handles. Gold-anchor marks. 11 inches high. *c.* 1785.

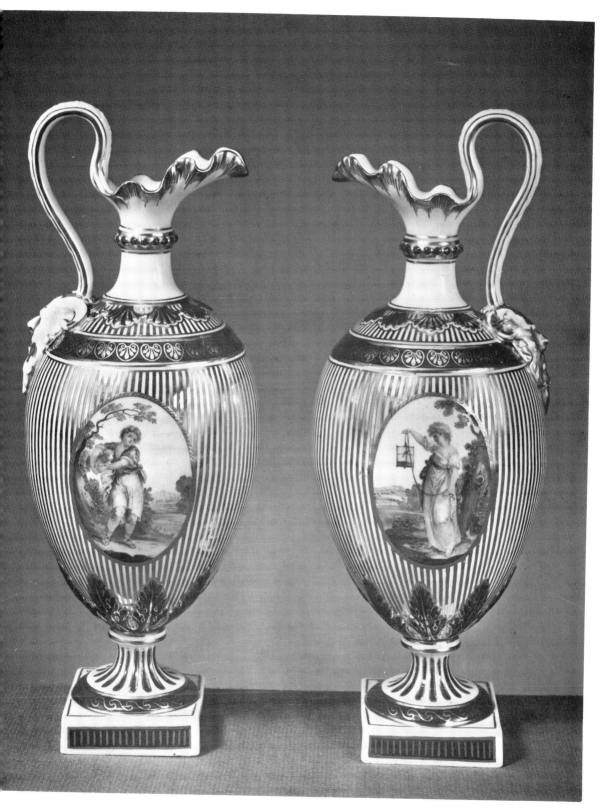

153 A documentary pair of Chelsea-Derby vases bearing the gold-anchor mark. These were included in the May 1781 sale of Derby and Chelsea porcelains and were described as 'A pair of uncommonly large octagon jars (near 2 feet high) decorated with natural flowers and finely enamel'd with figures, landscapes &c. richly ornamented with chas'd and burnished gold, the figures represent a votaress of Baccus and Innocence washing her hands at an altar'. 22 inches high.

Coalport

ALSO KNOWN AS 'COALBROOKDALE'
(c. 1796–present day)

At Coalport on the banks of the River Severn in Shropshire there were, early in the nineteenth century, two porcelain factories and one pottery factory (Walter Bradley & Co.). The porcelain factory normally associated with Coalport is that of John Rose. Called Rose Blakeway & Co., it was established by at least 1796, since records show that in August of that year the Prince and Princess of Orange visited the works. There is, however, some evidence that the firm was in existence early in 1793, and we even have a record of a letter sent to 'Mr. Rose, Manufactory, Salop' in June 1791, though this could relate to the nearby Caughley factory where John Rose received his training.

The earliest known examples from Rose's Coalport factory are the blue and white Coalport porcelain jugs (Plate 154) which relate to a Parliamentary election in 1796. Unfortunately the early pieces are unmarked, and in the past they have been incorrectly classed as Worcester or New Hall. In 1799 the successfully established Coalport partners purchased the Caughley factory on Thomas Turner's retirement (page 86). The Coalport partners continued to produce porcelains at the Caughley factory, and recent work on this site has enabled a vast range of John Rose & Co.'s wares of the 1800–1814 period to be positively identified. Plates 157–58, 160–62, and 171 show some of the site fragments with matching completed pieces. The early Coalport body is relatively hard and compact (it is, in fact, a type of hard-paste porcelain which tends to be thickly potted). Consequently examples feel heavy. However, the best means of identifying them is to study the basic shapes. Apart from the forms shown here, a very good range of key pieces will be found illustrated in my *Coalport and Coalbrookdale Porcelains* (Herbert Jenkins, London, 1970). The reader is warned, however, that the characteristic shapes were closely followed at the rival factory which traded as Anstice, Horton & Rose.

This partnership had the factory nearest the banks of the River Severn, opposite that of John Rose & Co., and separated from it only by a narrow canal. The rival manufactory was established in June 1800 by William Reynolds, William Horton, and Thomas Rose. In 1803, Robert Anstice joined Horton and Rose, following the death of William Reynolds,[1] and by the time of the dissolution of the Anstice, Horton & Rose partnership on February 1814, the series of Anstice pattern-numbers had reached 1419, while at the same period John Rose's numbers had not reached 500.

This information was kindly supplied by M. F. Messenger, F.L.A., Borough Library, Shrewsbury.

The Anstice factory was advertised for sale in February and March 1814 and was subsequently purchased by John Rose & Co., who closed the inconveniently placed Caughley factory and concentrated all their extensive activities on the Coalport site which now had two neighbouring works.

In the porcelain paste and styles of decoration the Anstice porcelains are extremely similar to those made by John Rose & Co., and the slight differences in the standard shapes afford the best guide to the maker (see Plates 165–66). Further details are given in my specialist book on Coalport porcelains.

After about 1814, when John Rose moved from Caughley and took over the Anstice factory opposite to his own original factory at Coalport, the porcelain and the covering glaze became softer and warmer to the touch—although there was still a tendency to thickly pot the plates and dishes. In 1820 John Rose won a Society of Arts Medal for his lead-free glaze, and for a period after this several different, circular printed marks occur. One such example is shown below:

As previously stated, the John Rose pattern-numbers after the first 1000 are expressed in fractional form, progressing through at least eight series, but the Anstice, Horton & Rose pattern-numbers run in simple sequence, reaching at least 1419 before the 1814 dissolution of the partnership.

It is hoped that a selection of Coalport porcelain will soon be displayed at the old factory at Coalport as part of the Ironbridge Gorge Museum Trust's work in preserving the industrial history of the district.

To many collectors the most characteristic type of Coalport porcelains are those richly decorated with encrusted flowers (Plates 183–85). This class is generally called 'Coalbrookdale'. Underglaze-blue marks occur on the earlier pieces of the 1820s and these marks include 'C Dale', 'C D', 'Coalbrookdale', and 'Coalport'. The later examples in this style are generally unmarked, but the shapes match those drawn in the travellers' design-book (see the *Illustrated Encyclopaedia of British Pottery and Porcelain*, Plate 170). It must not be thought, however, that all floral-encrusted porcelain of this type is Coalport, for most factories of the 1820–40 period made similar examples, particularly the Minton factory (Plate 382).

From about 1840 the potting became finer, as did the body, which was the standard nineteenth-century bone-china porcelain. Examples are seldom marked, but most table wares bear a painted pattern-number linking with the factory-records. The John Rose series of pattern-numbers runs from 1 to 1000. About 1820 a new series was started in fractional form 2/1 to 2/999, and after this in the mid-1830s a new series expressed over the number 3 was started and continued into at least an eighth series.

In 1875 the printed mark 'Coalport A.D. 1750' was introduced. This was superseded in 1881 by the following device which, with slight amendments—such as the addition of the word 'England' (in 1891) or 'Made in England' (from about 1920)—was continued until 1939. This standard Coalport mark was borne on all Coalport porcelains between 1881 and 1939, from white cups and saucers to a fine range of ornamental vases. Some of the basic shapes are shown in Plates 191 and 193. Such vases would be embellished with a variety of different ground colours, notably a rich, deep blue. The panels would be painted with scenes, figure-subjects, flowers, or fruit, by artists who, at this period, were permitted to sign their work. These later porcelains of the post-1880 period are at present highly regarded, for the quality of the painting is now almost impossible to equal and the second-hand specimens are far cheaper than modern examples.

In 1926 the Coalport firm was moved from Shropshire to the Staffordshire Potteries, where today, after several changes in ownership, it continues to uphold the high Coalport traditions, being since July 1967 part of the Wedgwood Group, although the Coalport name is retained.

As previously stated, the John Rose pattern-numbers after the first 1000 are expressed in fractional form, progressing to at least eight series, but the Anstice, Horton & Rose pattern-numbers run in simple sequence, reaching at least 1419 before the 1814 dissolution of the partnership.

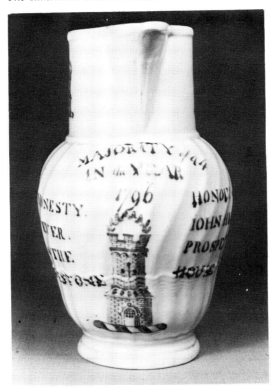

154 An early Coalport jug, dated 1796, relating to a local election. Unmarked. 8¾ inches high.

155 Two early Coalport jugs of characteristic shape, the smaller one printed in underglaze-blue with a typical Chinese-style landscape-design. 8¾ and 4¼ inches high. *c.* 1796–1800.

156 An early Coalport teapot of typical form bearing a so-called New Hall-enamelled design—but of a type favoured by most porcelain manufacturers of the period. 6½ inches high. *c.* 1800.

157 A blue-printed Coalport teapot of characteristic form, shown with related 'wasters' found on the Caughley factory-site—the Caughley works having been taken over by the Coalport partners in 1799.

158 Typical Coalport tea-ware
shapes of the early 1800s,
shown with 'wasters' from the
factory-site. The enamelled
'Bishop Sumner' pattern is
normally associated with the
Worcester factory but was
copied by other firms (see
Plate 104). Unmarked.
c. 1800–1803.

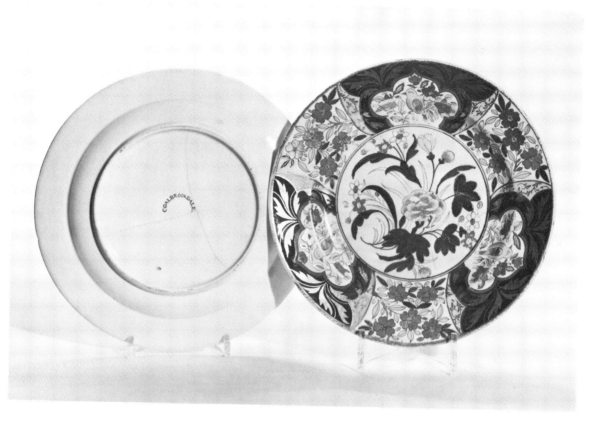

159 A typical Coalport 'Japan'-pattern plate, one reversed to show the rare 'Coalbrookdale' name-mark. *c.* 1805.

160 A Coalport 'Japan'-pattern plate of a popular design, shown with a 'waster' from the factory-site, bearing only the underglaze-blue portions of the design which would have been completed with overglaze enamels and gilding. *c.* 1805.

161 Characteristic Coalport
tea-ware shapes of the 1805
period, shown with 'wasters'
from the factory-site. The
dragon pattern is printed in
underglaze-blue. Teapot 6
inches high.

162 A blue-printed Coalport oval tureen, shown with unglazed fragments from the factory-site. Note the handle-forms. Tureen 12¼ inches long. *c.* 1805–10.

163 Typical early Coalport dinner-service forms of the 1805–10 period, including a complete oval tureen (Plate 162). Note the slightly lobbed dish- and plate-form.

opposite page
164 A Coalport ice-pail with liner and cover, decorated with a Worcester-styled design and scale-blue ground. Unmarked. 10½ inches high. *c.* 1805–10.

165 Similar teapots from the two rival Coalport factories. The top example is from the Anstice Horton & Rose factory, the lower one by John Rose & partners. This bears the pattern number 315 which agrees with the factory pattern book entry. 10 inches long. *c.* 1810–14.

166 The left-hand sugar-basin was made by the Anstice, Horton & Rose partners at Coalport, the right-hand example is of John Rose's manufacture. Note the differing knob-forms and the form of the mask handles. *c.* 1810.

167 A rare Anstice, Horton & Rose Coalport covered sugar-basin of the 1810 period. Note the knob-shape. 5½ inches high.

168 A decorative Anstice, Horton & Rose Coalport teapot. A very similar-shaped pot was made by the rival John Rose factory, but note this characteristic Anstice knob. 6½ inches high. *c.* 1810.

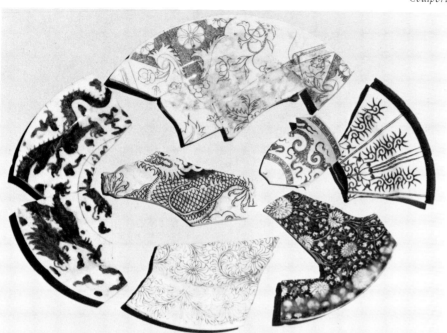

169 A selection of Coalport (John Rose) factory 'wasters', showing some typical printed designs of the 1800–1810 period.

170 An unmarked Coalport cup and saucer, shown with th corresponding page from the John Rose pattern-book. The pattern-books and finds on the factory-site have enabled much unmarked porcelain to be attributed to Coalport.

171 Two John Rose unmarked
jugs, shown with unglazed
pieces of the handle and half of
the plaster mould for such a
handle. Similar jugs with a
slightly different handle were
made by the Anstice, Horton
& Rose partnership. Covered
jug 8¼ inches high. *c.* 1810–15.

172 A charming Coalport teapot of a rare form decorated with an overglaze 'bat'-print. 6½ inches high. *c.* 1815.

173 A noble John Rose teapot decorated with the popular Coalport green-dragon pattern. 6¾ inches high. *c.* 1810.

74 Two typical, unmarked
Coalport pieces,
commemorating George IV's
Jubilee in 1809. 4½ inches high.

75 Two unmarked Coalport
jardinières, shown with related
fragments from the factory-
site. 6¾ and 5¼ inches high.
1805–10.

176 Typical Coalport tea wares of the 1820–25 period, of pattern-number 986, agreeing with the John Rose factory pattern-book. Teapot 6½ inches high.

177 A John Rose Coalport creamer with relief-moulded floral design and painted in a typical manner. Printed 1820 Society of Arts mark. 4¼ inches high. *c.* 1820.

178 A finely painted dessert centrepiece, showing to good effect the relief-moulded design—as Plate 177. 12 × 8¾ inches. *c.* 1818–22.

179 Representative pieces from a John Rose Coalport dessert set of the 1820s painted in a characteristic manner—the central spray with an escaping tulip. Unmarked. Centrepiece 5¼ inches high.

166

180 A superb Coalport dessert service of the 1820 period, showing again the moulded design seen in Plates 177–78. Ice-pails 12$\frac{1}{2}$ inches high.

181 A good-quality Coalport teapot of the mid-1820s of a characteristic shape. 6¾ inches high.

182 A good Coalport creamer, the flower-painting by J. Birbeck. Marked with the fractional pattern-number $\frac{3}{113}$. 4½ inches high. *c.* 1840.

opposite page
183 A good and typical floral-encrusted pot-pourri vase in the style known as 'Coalbrookdale', but not all such pieces are of Coalport make. 11 inches high. *c.* 1840. The original price was £3.3.0

184 A rare 'Coalbrookdale' toy pot. 3¾ inches high. *c.* 1830.

185 A typical, floral-encrusted, 'Coalbrookdale' covered bowl of the 1825–35 period. Within recent years the Coalport firm have re-introduced this style. 4¾ inches high.

186 A superbly painted
Coalport dessert service,
showing typical shapes of the
1840s. This set bears the
fractional pattern-number $\frac{4}{257}$,
attributed in the factory
pattern-book to the painter
Stephen Lawrence. Comport
$8\frac{1}{4}$ inches high.

187 A turquoise-ground Coalport vase painted with Sèvres-type birds by John Randall. Ampersand mark. 13¾ inches high. *c.* 1870.

188 A Coalport cup and saucer of the 1870s painted in a typical manner with John Randall's birds.

189 A turquoise-ground
Coalport vase decorated in the
Sèvres-style and bearing the
C.B.D. monogram-mark of the
1851–61 period. 12 inches high.

opposite page
190 A superb-quality yellow-ground Coalport vase, richly gilt. The panel signed by Thomas Keeling. Printed crowned 'Coalport A.D. 1750' mark. 12 inches high. *c.* 1905.

191 A selection of Coalport vase-shapes reproduced from a catalogue of the early 1900s.

192 Three typical Coalport vases of the 1910–20 period. The centre vase is by the fruit-painter C. H. Chivers, the scenic vases by E. O. Ball. Each is signed. Printed crowned 'Coalport A.D. 1750' mark. 15½ and 14 inches high.

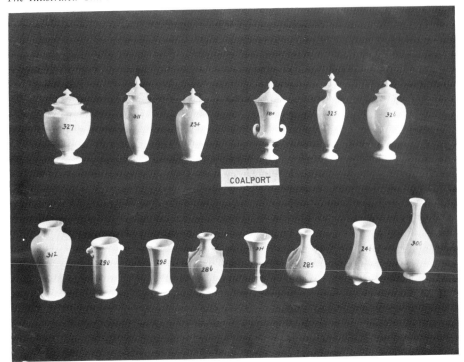

193 Further Coalport vase-shapes reproduced from a catalogue of the early 1900s.

194 Coalport shapes from the factory record-book, showing the standard mark on the left with the post-1891 addition of the word 'England'.

Copeland & Garrett and Copeland

COPELAND & GARRETT AND COPELAND
(1833–1970)

On 1 March 1833 the Copeland & Garrett partnership succeeded the long-established Spode concern at Stoke (see page 384). In general, the new firm continued the old Spode lines and styles, and there is no clear-cut demarcation line between the products of the two. Well-tried, traditional patterns were continued, seemingly with success. In many cases the marks of the new partnership were the only means of differentiating between the porcelains (or the various earthenwares) of Spode and Copeland & Garrett, at least in the 1830s.

In the early 1840s, however, Messrs Copeland & Garrett introduced their 'statuary porcelain' or 'Parian' (page 341)—a body that is typically Victorian, and which was to be taken up by practically every British porcelain manufacturer.

One of the Copeland & Garrett specialities comprised large plaques, some of which were made for fireplace surrounds. Good animal models were also made, and all their porcelains display quality of workmanship. The marks incorporate the names Copeland & Garrett or the initials C & G. Sample marks are shown.

The Copeland & Garrett pattern-numbers are progressive, following on from the Spode sequence. The new numbers commence at about 5700 and continue to approximately 7200. Some few underglaze-blue pattern-numbers bear the prefix B. These make up a separate series which runs from about B.400. It must be remembered that some marked Copeland & Garrett wares will bear earlier pattern-numbers, first introduced in the Spode period.

COPELAND

Messrs W. T. Copeland succeeded the Copeland & Garrett partnership in 1847. The Spode tradition of fine-quality porcelain was continued (earthenwares were also made). This is especially seen in the high standard of the painting and gilding (Plates 200, 205–6). In contrast to the richly decorated wares, the matt white Parian figures, groups, and busts formed a most important aspect of Copeland's output. Such pieces bear the impressed name-mark 'COPELAND'.

Several of Copeland's talented artists signed their work. Examples by Samuel Alcock (Plate 206), Lucien Besche, C. F. Hurten (Plate 203), Daniel Lucas (Plates 199 and 200), T. Worral (Plate 205), and James Weaver are especially noteworthy. The standard Copeland marks included this name, and the mark shown is that

177

COPELAND

normally found on porcelains from about 1851. The wording 'Spode. Copeland's China, England' appears on wares made after 1891.

In 1970 the story turned full circle when the firm of W. T. Copeland & Sons Ltd took the new style 'Spode Ltd', so cementing the link with the original Spode firm.

The nineteenth-century pattern-numbers are progressive, rather than fractional. The old Spode and Copeland & Garrett sequence was continued until 9999 in about 1852. Subsequently a new series with the prefix D was used, ranging to D.9999 in the late 1870s. Then the porcelain pattern-numbers were prefixed 1/ (the earthenwares had the prefix 2/), and this series had reached 1/9929 by January 1900.

195 A typically rather ornate
Copeland & Garrett vase,
illustrating the continuation of
the former Spode quality.
Printed name-mark with
pattern-number 6134. 10 inches
high. *c.* 1840.

196 A superb presentation
Copeland & Garrett cup and
saucer decorated in the
richest manner. Diameter of
saucer 6 inches. Special printed
name-mark, with date, 13–14
November 1834.

197 A typical moulded Copeland jug, the design registered in November 1849. Diamond-shaped registration-mark. 6 inches high.

198 A comport from a typical Copeland dessert service of the mid-1840s. The Copeland floral painting is most effective. Printed mark and pattern-number 8390. 8 inches high.

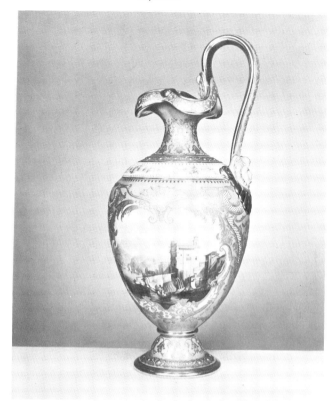

199 A large Copeland vase, the panel painted by Daniel Lucas. This piece was shown at the 1862 Exhibition. Impressed and printed name-marks. 23½ inches high.

200 A fine-quality Copeland ewer, richly gilt and jewelled, painted by Daniel Lucas. This example was shown at the 1851 Exhibition. 15¼ inches high.

201 A moulded Parian jug, the reliefs depicting the landing of Columbus in America. Impressed name-mark with 'England'. 8 inches high. *c.* 1895.

202 A pair of fine-quality Copeland Parian figures, representing thousands of models produced by this firm in the 1840s (see page 341). Impressed name-mark. 9½ inches high. *c.* 1865.

203 A powerfully painted, large plaque by the German artist C. F. Hurten, signed at the top-left corner. Copelands produced many large plaques and panels. 24 × 18 inches. *c.* 1875.

204 A fine-quality Copeland plate of the 1850s, decorated in the Sèvres style. Printed mark. Diameter 9 inches.

183

opposite page
205 An important and finely painted and gilt vase, the flower-painting signed by J. Worral. Printed mark 'Copeland's China England'. 17½ inches high. *c.* 1910.

206 A superbly gilt Copeland vase of large size, painted in the typical manner of the Royal Academy-trained artist Samuel Alcock. 31 inches high. *c.* 1890.

Daniel

HENRY & RICHARD DANIEL
(1822–45)

The Daniel porcelains are related to the sumptuous Spode wares in that Henry Daniel and his team of enamellers and gilders had an independent decorating establishment within the Spode works at Stoke-on-Trent. Here they decorated all Spode porcelain before the arrangement was terminated by mutual consent in August 1822.

By July 1823 Henry Daniel had taken over Joseph Poulson's factory at Stoke, and in March 1827 additional premises were acquired at Shelton. Henry Daniel was joined by his elder son Richard, and until 1826 they traded as 'Daniel & Son', this style being then amended to 'Henry & Richard Daniel'. These names appear rarely as painted or printed marks.

The Daniel porcelain is relatively soft; there is a tendency to cracking and the glaze is very often crazed. The shapes are unusual and quite characteristic (see Plates 207, 208 and 212–13) and the decoration is particularly fine, as one would expect from a firm which had been responsible for decorating the Spode porcelains. The gilding is extremely rich, often combining matt gold with burnished gilding. Raised gilt work was sometimes employed.

Some of the first Daniel porcelains were made for the local patron of the Staffordshire Potters, the Earl of Shrewsbury. S. Shaw noted in his *History of the Staffordshire Potteries*, published in 1829, that, 'Early in 1827 Messrs. Daniel completed for the Earl of Shrewsbury different services of porcelain of the most brilliant and costly kind ever manufactured in the district. . . .' Pieces from the Shrewsbury services are shown in Plates 207 and 208, and these are really magnificent porcelains.

One of the Daniel specialities was ornately enamelled armorial bearings. A plate from a harlequin service, the pieces having differently coloured borders, is shown in Plate 209, and two other typically fine specimens are shown in my *Illustrated Encyclopaedia of British Pottery and Porcelain* (Plates 188–89).

Henry Daniel died in April 1841 at a time when two hundred and forty people were employed at the works. Richard Daniel continued at Stoke to at least 1845. Identification depends on a knowledge of key shapes. The Daniel pattern-numbers are of the simple progressive type ranging to about 9000. For further information the reader is referred to Michael Berthoud's specialist book *H & R Daniel 1822–1846*, (Micawber, 1980).

207 A tureen-stand from one of the magnificent services made for the Earl of Shrewsbury in 1827, bearing the Earl's crest in the centre. The fine, green ground is richly gilt and inset with hand-painted paneis. These richly decorated Daniel services may be likened to the finest Spode wares. Printed mark as reproduced on the opposite page. $14\frac{1}{2} \times$ 13 inches.

208 One of the Shrewsbury dessert plates, showing a characteristic Daniel shape. Diameter 8½ inches. *c.* 1827.

209 A fine-quality Daniel porcelain plate made for the Earl of Shrewsbury's daughter on her marriage in 1839. Printed name-mark. Diameter 9½ inches.

210 Two Daniel porcelain saucers, one reversed to show the painted name-mark 'H & R Daniel, Stoke-upon-Trent, Staffordshire'. Diameter $5\frac{3}{4}$ inches. *c.* 1830.

211 A large-size Daniel cabinet-cup and saucer rather in the Spode manner but with the painted Daniel name-mark. Diameter of saucer $6\frac{1}{2}$ inches. *c.* 1830.

following 2 pages
212 A maroon-ground richly gilt Daniel porcelain vase of the 1830s and of characteristic shape. $9\frac{1}{2}$ inches high.

213 Representative pieces from a Daniel tea service of the 1830s, showing characteristic and identifying forms. Marked only with the pattern-number 4496. Diameter of plate 9 inches.

Davenport

DAVENPORT
(c. 1793–1887)

Firstly, it must be made clear that Davenport is a family- and not a place-name, and that such descriptions as 'made at Davenport' are incorrect. The Davenport factory or, rather, factories (four separate works existed) were situated at Longport (Burslem) in the Staffordshire Potteries. The concern was reputedly established by John Davenport in 1793, but the early wares were no doubt restricted to pottery—the known porcelain wares all appear to be of nineteenth-century date.

Very little is recorded about the pre-1830 Davenport porcelains, and marked specimens are surprisingly rare. However, those that are known show the high quality of these porcelains, which are of a compact, refined body. When marks occur they comprise the word 'Davenport' in curved form over an anchor device (see Plate 220). Some wares bear the painted place-name 'Longport' and these are believed to be of Davenport origin.

The post-1830 Davenport porcelains closely follow in general style the Coalport wares (for example, dessert services were often painted with landscape views). The standard mark of the 1830–70 period is shown. This normally appears printed in underglaze-blue, signifying a date in the 1850–70 period. Another standard mark was the crown over the words 'Davenport. Longport. Staffordshire' (arranged in three lines).

Some painted plaques occur bearing the impressed words 'Davenports Patent'. Such plaques were sold to independent decorators in large numbers in the 1860–80 period, and such painting on marked Davenport plaques is not necessarily factory work. Attractive scenic paintings signed by Richard Ablott are to be found on these marked Davenport plaques.

The Davenport firm became a limited liability company in 1881, but this failed in 1887. It must be remembered that the bulk of the Davenport output before 1860 comprised earthenwares of various types. The reader is referred to T. Lockett's and G. Godden's specialist joint book, *Davenport: China, Earthenware & Glass 1794-1887* (Barrie & Jenkins, London, 1989). The reader is also referred to Mr Lockett's contribution to *Staffordshire Porcelain* (Granada, 1983), chapter 10.

The Davenport pattern-numbers followed a simple progressive sequence, but this probably did not exceed seven thousand—an example bearing an 1856 registration-mark bears the relatively low pattern-number 1174.

214 A Davenport porcelain tureen from an attractive dessert service. Impressed mark as Plate 220. 6¾ inches high. *c.* 1810.

215 A Davenport porcelain bulb-pot, the pierced, flat cover missing. Impressed mark as Plate 220. 5 inches high. *c.* 1810.

216 An early Davenport
porcelain dessert dish, the
painting traditionally attributed
to Thomas Steel. Painted
'Davenport-Longport' mark.
c. 1805–10.

opposite page
217 Representative pieces from
a Davenport porcelain dessert
service of the 1810 period.
Impressed mark as Plate 220.
Centrepiece 6¼ inches high.

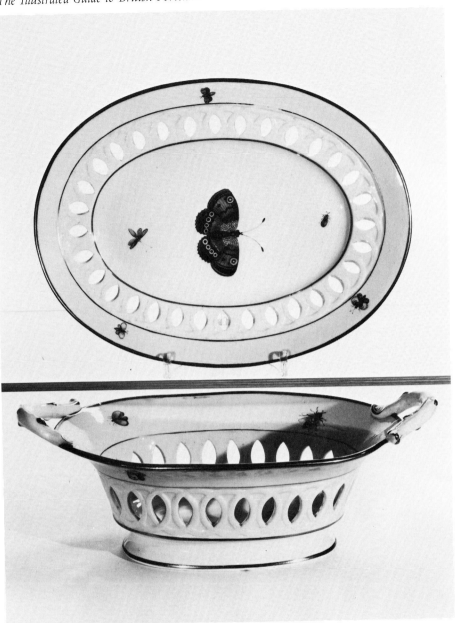

218 One of a pair of fruit-baskets and stands from a dessert service of the 1810 period. The centrepiece is shown in Plate 219. Basket 11½ inches long.

219 A Davenport porcelain centrepiece from a dessert service, attractively painted with butterflies and moths, with simple gilt-line borders. *c.* 1810. 6 inches high.

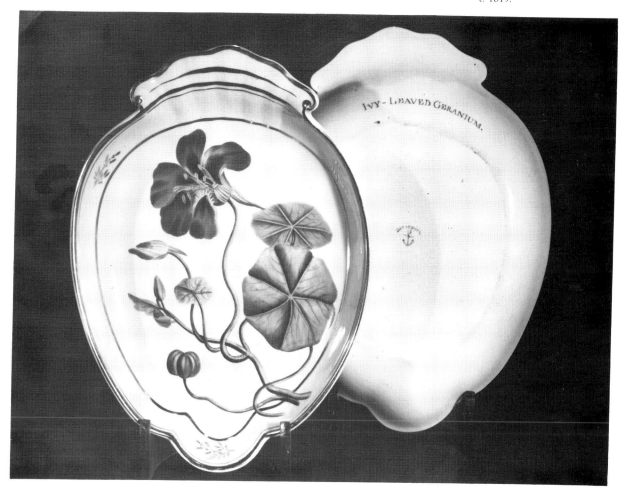

220 Two-handled dishes from a magnificent dessert service painted with named flowers. The standard impressed mark is shown in the centre of the reversed dish. $8\frac{3}{4} \times 6\frac{1}{2}$ inches. *c.* 1815.

IVY - LEAVED GERANIUM.

221 A superb-quality Davenport cup and saucer, the cup with gilt interior. Printed 'Longport' mark. Diameter of saucer 5 inches. *c.* 1820.

222 A superbly decorated Davenport plate which in the fine bone-china body, as well as in the decoration, rivals similar examples from any factory—including Swansea. Printed anchor and 'Davenport' mark, pattern-number 170. Diameter $9\frac{3}{4}$ inches. *c.* 1820.

opposite page
223 A green-bordered Davenport porcelain dessert service, the landscape centres painted in the manner of Jesse Mountford. The shapes are typical of the late 1840s. Printed mark 'Davenport. Longport, Staffordshire' under a crown. Pattern-number 841. Comport $8\frac{1}{2}$ inches high.

224 A Davenport porcelain low-covered vase decorated with a 'Japan' pattern. In shape and style of decoration this is a copy of a Derby original, but many late Davenport designs closely follow the Derby patterns. Printed mark as Plate 223. 5¾ inches high. *c.* 1860–70.

Derby

DERBY
(*c.* 1750–present day)

Porcelain has been produced in the city of Derby for over two hundred years, but not by a single company or even on the original factory-site. Almost from the start the aim was high, and one finds ornamental figures and groups, also fine vases, being made in preference to table wares—in fact, the factory in the eighteenth century styled itself the 'second Dresden'. These aims and ambitions were to a large degree fulfilled, and it is to the management's credit that at this early period they did not mark their 'second Dresden' porcelains with that factory's well-known crossed-swords mark. Indeed, before about 1780 the Derby porcelains are very seldom marked at all.

The key man in the story of Derby porcelain is William Duesbury, although the somewhat mysterious Andrew Planche 'china-maker' almost certainly had an important, but largely unknown, part in the story. William Duesbury was by trade an enameller of various types of salt-glazed stoneware and early porcelains, practising his craft in London between 1750 (or earlier) and 1753. At this period porcelain was already being made at Derby. Some few white jugs bear the date 1750 (see the *Illustrated Encyclopaedia of British Pottery and Porcelain*, Plate 211) and Duesbury's 1750–53 account-book includes references to 'Darbey' figures. It is believed that these early examples were produced by Heath & Company (John Heath and Andrew Planche). The two amusing little figures representing Air and Water (Plate 225) belong to this period soon after 1750 and illustrate early characterisation. They are slip-cast (see page 19) and therefore relatively light in weight. The base is free of glaze, and the edge has in this case been cleaned up with a knife, although normally it can be seen that the glaze stops short of the base, leaving a 'dry edge' or rim. The glaze is whitish rather than glass-like due to an opaquefying agent such as tin-oxide. The vent-hole under the base usually appears to be countersunk —like a screw hole.

By an unsigned agreement dated 1 January 1756, 'William Duesbury of Longton (Staffordshire) Enammelor' agreed to join with John Heath and Andrew Planche as co-partners to produce 'English China', and from this time until his death in 1786 William Duesbury was the dominant partner. The products of the 1756–60 period have rather pale colouring and a general lack of gilding—the Dresden-style basket-figure shown here as Plate 226 is a typical example. A class of large vase, decorated with a rich, streaky blue ground is reasonably common (Plates 230–31). Vases of this type were once thought to be Longton Hall.

Useful wares are quite rare in pre-1770 Derby porcelain; the few surviving specimens are usually enamelled with Chinese-style figure-subjects (Plates 232–33) or with floral designs. Examples decorated in underglaze-blue again show Oriental influence (Plates 234 and 236–37). These useful wares as well as the figures, groups, and vases normally show three or more dark "patch marks" or "pad-marks" where the piece was supported in the kiln (Plates 241, 248, also Plates 146 and 149). These porcelains are unmarked, although some pieces bear a copy of the Chelsea mark. Pad-marks can rarely occur on Chelsea pieces.

From 1770 to 1785 William Duesbury's Derby Company also ran the Chelsea factory in London, and this aspect of Derby porcelain is considered separately on page 139.

Both at Chelsea and at Derby at this period factory-marks were introduced. At Derby the most common mark during approximately the 1770–82 period was the crown with a cursive D below; this device was often painted in a blue enamel. The use of the crown device probably gave rise to the comparatively recent term 'Crown Derby'. In about 1782 the famous 'baton' mark was introduced. This comprises the crown and the D, but with the crossed batons, with dots at each end. This basic mark remained in use for many years, up to about 1825. Up to 1805, it was very neatly painted in puce, blue, or—rarely—black. Afterwards it appears in red enamel and is rather carelessly drawn. (See below.)

This crowned-baton mark was also incised into the underside of figures, particularly the rightly famous, superb-quality Derby biscuit figures and groups (Plates 247–49) which were introduced in about 1771 and remained in production through the early years of the nineteenth century. (See T. Clifford's paper 'Derby Biscuit', published in the *Transactions of the English Ceramic Circle*, Vol. 7, Part 2, 1969.)

Returning to table wares, the really magnificent Derby porcelains of the puce- and blue-mark period, that is *c.* 1782–1805, are of a warm, waxy body, covered with a lovely, mellow, whitened glaze, which sometimes shows scum-marks at the edges, see Plate 256. These delicately painted wares (Plates 250–58) were decorated by a team of highly talented artists—including the famous William Billingsley—and they are amongst the most pleasing ever produced. After William Duesbury's death in 1786 the works were continued by his son of the same name, who died in 1796. After this, the factory was continued by Michael Kean until the Bloor period.

After about 1805 when the mark appears painted in red enamel, the decoration tends to be more pretentious (Plates 259–61, 264–67, and Colour Plate V) although always of good quality. The ever-popular 'Japan' patterns with areas of underglaze-blue in conjunction with overglaze-enamel and gilding also date from this red-mark period. Good examples of two traditional Derby 'Japan' patterns are shown in Plates 262–63. With the advent of the red mark the glaze becomes rather thicker and transparent but is very prone to crazing and discoloration.

Between 1811 and 1815 the Derby factory was acquired by Robert Bloor. For some years he employed the old Crown Derby mark, apparently not using the first of his own marks until the 1820s. These Bloor marks are reproduced below.

The term 'Bloor Derby' is normally only applied to these later pieces bearing his marks, and in general such pieces are held in little regard. Some Bloor-period Derby porcelain is of very fine quality (see Plate 269), but the prevailing taste of that period and the need to cut costs and sell slightly faulty pieces justifies the loss of favour. The Bloor-Derby porcelains also suffered from increasing competition from the many Staffordshire firms that turned their attention to the manufacture of porcelain. In 1848 the original Derby factory in Nottingham Road closed. The subsequent history of Derby porcelain is continued on page 229.

Pattern-numbers seldom appear on Derby porcelain. When they do they are found under the basic crowned-baton mark during the period *c.* 1782–1820; they are not found on earlier examples and very seldom on marked Bloor-Derby porcelain. Porcelain bearing only a pattern-number will not be of Derby origin.

Most general reference-books give an outline history of Derby porcelain; several specialist books deal in detail with the wares and its decorators. In general, all subsequent works draw heavily on one Victorian work written by a former Derby painter, John Haslem. This, now scarce, book is *The Old Derby China Factory, the Workmen and their Productions* (George Bell & Sons, London, 1876). Later specialist works include: *Crown Derby Porcelain* by F. Brayshaw Gilhespy (F. Lewis, Leigh-on-Sea, 1951), *Derby Porcelain* by F. Brayshaw Gilhespy (MacGibbon & Kee, London, 1961), *Derby Porcelain* by F. A. Barrett and A. L. Thorpe (Faber & Faber, London, 1971), also *Royal Crown Derby* by John Twitchett & Betty Bailey (Third edition, Antique Collectors' Club, 1988). The Derby Museum and Art Gallery contains an excellent array of local porcelains, as does the Museum attached to the factory of the present Royal Crown Derby Porcelain Co. Ltd.

225 Two early Derby slip-cast porcelain figures of Chinese boys, representing Air and Water, the latter turned to show the incised name and a typical unglazed base. 4 inches high. *c.* 1750–52.

226 An early Derby basket-figure, one of a pair showing typical pale colouring. Pad-marks under base. $8\frac{7}{8}$ inches high. *c.* 1755–60.

227 A pair of early Derby vases of a characteristic shape, the flower-painting being typical. Note especially the thin, cotton-like stems. 9 inches high. *c.* 1755–60.

205

228 A white Derby figure of a lamp-lighter or night watchman with unusual form of base. 5½ inches high. *c.* 1760.

229 An attractive Derby group of the early 1760s, crisply modelled and painted in a typical style. 6¾ inches high.

230 A blue-ground Derby
covered vase of a type formerly
thought to be Longton Hall.
Pad-marks under base. $10\frac{1}{4}$
inches high. *c.* 1758–60.

231 Two Derby side-vases
similar to the centre example
shown above. The style of
bird-painting is especially
characteristic. Pad-marks under
base. $8\frac{1}{4}$ inches high. *c.*
1758–60.

207

232 An attractive, naïvely
painted Derby porcelain coffee
pot, with typical handle-form.
9 inches high. *c.* 1755–60.

233 A Derby creamer
enamelled in the popular
Oriental style. Derby tea wares
of the 1750s and 1760s are
comparatively rare. Pad-marks
under base $2\frac{9}{10}$ inches high.
c. 1760.

234 A Derby openwork basket, painted in underglaze-blue in the fashionable Oriental style. 9½ inches long. *c.* 1758–62.

235 A Derby bowl with pierced cover painted in underglaze-blue. This is a characteristic Derby form. Pad-marks under base. 7¼ inches high. *c.* 1758–62.

236 A rare form of relief-
moulded Derby oval butter-dish,
painted in underglaze-blue.
5 × 4¼ inches. *c.* 1760.

237 A Derby, lobed tureen and
cover painted in a bright
underglaze-blue. A similar
form was also made at the Bow
factory. 5¾ inches long.
c. 1760.

238 An attractive Derby group after a Dresden model taken from the Italian Comedy. Pad-marks under base. 12 inches high. *c.* 1758–60.

239 Three Derby bird models. The reader should note that similar examples were made at Bow and at Chelsea as well as at many later factories. 5 and $4\frac{5}{8}$ inches high. *c.* 1770.

240 A typical Derby model of
Neptune, a popular figure made
over many years. Pad-marks
under base. 9½ inches high.
c. 1770.

241 Two seated Seasons, one
turned to show a typical
Derby base with circular pad-
marks. 6 inches high. *c.* 1770.

opposite page
242 A typical Derby figure of
the 1770s of a type often
referred to as Chelsea-Derby,
but it appears to be wholly of
Derby make. Note the
beginnings of the scroll-footed
base. Pad-marks. 10 inches
high.

212

243 A magnificent dessert dish from a service made for the Duke of Hamilton. Pieces from this set bear the rare enamelled mark, 'Duesbury London', relating to the London showroom. The more usual cursive initial N has been incised into the body. $9\frac{7}{8}$ inches. *c.* 1780.

244 Two unmarked Derby duck sauce-boats. The May 1778 auction sale included 'Pair duck boats with a brown edge'. Enamelled examples were included in subsequent sales. 4 inches high. *c.* 1778–85.

245 A charming Derby, lobed teapot decorated with overglaze 'Smiths' blue and gilding, in the neo-classical taste much favoured at Derby. Crowned 'D' mark in puce. 5¼ inches high. *c.* 1775–80.

246 A tasteful Derby 'monteith', in which wine-glasses were cooled or rinsed, the glasses hanging by the foot inwards into water. Crowned 'D' mark in blue enamel. 13½ inches long. *c.* 1780–85.

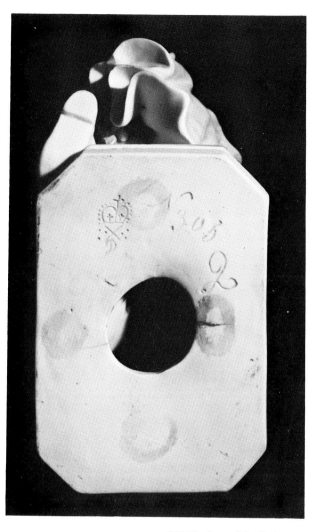

248 The base of the Derby
bisque figure shown right.
Note the four dark pad-marks,
the standard crowned 'D' and
crossed-baton mark—incised
in this case—and the model-
number 305. The number 2
refers to the second size, for all
such models were made in
differing sizes.

249 A Derby bisque figure of
Shakespeare, a popular model,
much copied at other factories.
Note the slight sheen to the
Derby body. The base and
typical marks are shown left.
10 inches high. *c.* 1790.

opposite page
247 A fine-quality and typical
Derby bisque (unglazed)
porcelain group. Marked with
model-number 235 incised. 14¾
inches high. *c.* 1785.

250 A charming Derby teapot of a delightfully warm, waxy-feeling body and glaze. The landscape-panel and tastefully gilt border are quite typical. Crowned 'D' and crossed-batons mark in blue enamel, with pattern-number 137. 6¼ inches high. *c.* 1790.

251 A rare and finely painted Derby cabaret service with apple-green ground. The seascapes are a rare and desirable form of decoration favoured at the Derby factory. Blue-enamel mark as Plate 250 above. *c.* 1790–95.

252 A rare form of Derby monteith bowl (see Plate 246) from a large special service. The cornflower-like design was popular at this factory in the 1790–1810 period. Crowned 'D' mark with crossed batons in puce enamel. 4¾ inches high. *c.* 1790–95.

253 Representative pieces from a superb-quality Derby service, including the ice-pail, a cream-tureen, and a sample plate. The rose-painting on the friendly soft-glaze is charming. Some pieces have the incised, cursive initial N, others the standard crowned mark in puce or blue enamel, and some pieces have the gold-anchor mark. Ice-pail 9½ inches high. *c.* 1790–95.

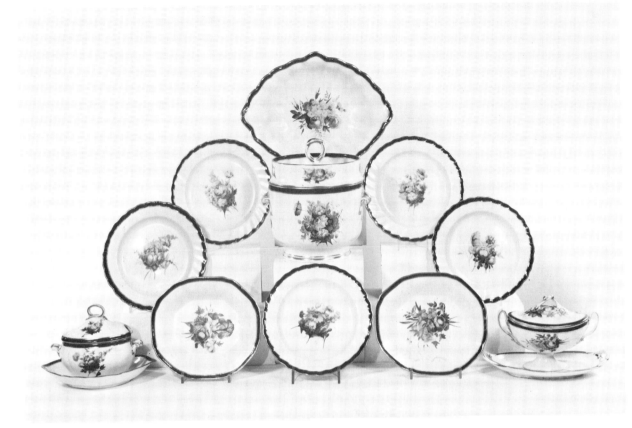

254 Representative pieces of a Derby dessert service, finely painted with flowers. Crowned 'D' mark with crossed batons, with pattern-numbers 100 and 127 in blue. *c.* 1780–90.

255 A green-bordered Derby sprig-pattern tureen, cover, and stand. Puce-painted mark as Plate 254. Tureen 5¾ inches high. *c.* 1785–95.

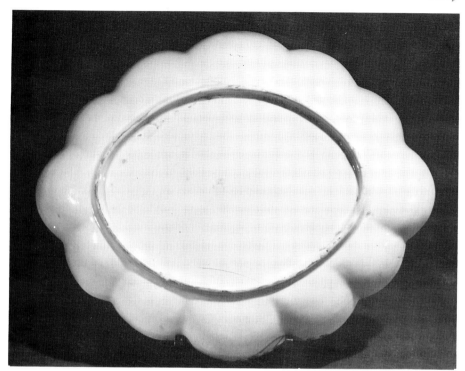

256 The reverse of a dish from the dessert set in Plate 255, showing the neatly painted factory-mark in puce enamel. Note also the way the glaze has not covered parts of the foot-rim, leaving darker portions. $11\frac{1}{4} \times 9$ inches. *c.* 1785–95.

257 A superb, large Derby tureen, painted with flowers in the style of William (Quaker) Pegg. Length 18 inches. *c.* 1795–1800.

221

258 An attractive Derby scenic-panelled flower-vase with separate cover. Rare pale-yellow ground. Crowned 'D' and batons mark in blue enamel. 7 inches high. *c.* 1795–1800.

259 A pair of two-piece blue-ground vases painted with views in the manner of George Robertson. Blue mark as Plate 258. 8¼ inches high. *c.* 1800.

260 A finely gilt Derby ice-pail, shown with the cover off; the inner liner is in this case missing. Standard crowned 'D' mark with crossed batons, in red. Base. 5¾ inches high. *c.* 1815.

261 Representative parts of a superb Derby dessert service with pierced openwork edges. These shapes are, however, extremely rare and not representative of the standard shapes. Crowned 'D' mark with crossed batons in red. Ice-pails 13¼ inches high. *c.* 1815.

262 A typical Derby 'Japan'-pattern tureen, cover, and stand. This is a basic tureen shape of the 1820s, a pair being in each dessert service and two or more in a dinner service. This standard 'Japan' pattern in underglaze-blue, with red and green enamels, and gilt enrichments occurs on a wide range of Derby porcelains, but several other factories issued very similar designs. Standard red-painted mark. $5\frac{1}{4}$ inches high.

263 A rare Derby coffee-pot form of the early 1820s, illustrating a further standard Derby 'Japan' pattern. In this case the gilt enrichments and the whole design are carefully painted, but such standard 'Japan' patterns are of variable quality and many examples were painted by semi-skilled hands. Crowned 'D' mark with crossed batons in red. $9\frac{1}{2}$ inches high.

opposite page
264 Representative pieces from a scenic-painted Derby dessert service, with typical, ornate gilt border. Standard red-painted mark. Tureen $6\frac{1}{2}$ inches high. *c.* 1820.

265 Representative pieces from a Derby dessert service, the bird-painted centres probably by Richard Dodson. Note the typical, ornate gilt borders. Standard red-painted mark. *c.* 1820.

266 A dessert dish from a fine-quality service, the centre panels painted by Thomas Steel, a talented artist who later worked for Mintons (see Plates 379–81). Standard red-painted mark. $9\frac{3}{4} \times 7\frac{1}{2}$ inches. *c.* 1820–25.

267 Representative pieces from a dessert set painted by Thomas Steel (see above). This grouping shows typical Derby dessert shapes of the 1820–30 period. Standard red-painted mark. Tureens $5\frac{1}{4}$ inches high.

268 The side- and handle-form of the coffee-can shown opposite.

269 A Bloor-Derby coffee-can, showing both the quality that could be attained at this late period and also the habit of copying earlier styles. Circular 'Bloor-Derby' mark in red. $2\frac{1}{2}$ inches high. *c.* 1830–34.

270 A floral-encrusted Bloor-Derby blue-ground ewer. Crown mark with 'Derby' below in red. 13½ inches high. *c.* 1840–48.

271 A floral-encrusted Bloor-Derby lavender-water sprinkler. Circular 'Bloor-Derby' mark in red. 3½ inches high. *c.* 1835–40.

Derby-King Street Works

KING STREET WORKS
(1848–1935)

On the closure of the original Derby porcelain factory in Nottingham Road in 1848, several of the employees grouped together to purchase some of the remaining working materials and set up a small works in King Street, Derby, to continue the old traditions. The King Street products follow very closely the shapes and patterns established at the old factory, and the old Derby factory-mark was sometimes copied, but with crossed swords under the crown, rather than the crossed batons of the original.

Rarely one finds printed marks relating to the changing trade names—'Locker & Co, Late Bloor' (1849–59), 'Stevenson, Sharp & Co' (1859–61), or 'Courtney, Late Bloor'—the last relates to the retail shop at 34 Old Bond Street. In 1861 Llewellynn Jewitt designed a new trade-mark, being in effect the old red Derby Crown, crossed batons (now changed to swords) and 'D' device with the initials S and H added, one each side. These initials stood for the then partners Stevenson and Hancock. It is not generally realised that this mark was used from 1861 continuously to 1935 when the King Street firm was merged with the Royal Crown Derby Company, although sometimes the initials were not added. The concern was a relatively small one, and it appears that at times porcelains were purchased in the white from Staffordshire and merely decorated at the King Street works. Plates 273–74 reproduce two pages from the firm's catalogue of the 1920s, showing some of the old Crown Derby-style products.

The reader is referred to the specialist book *Royal Crown Derby* (Third edition, Antique Collectors' Club, 1988).

272 A pair of Stevenson &
Hancock Derby bisque figures
after earlier Derby originals.
Incised mark. 6¾ inches high.
c. 1865.

273 A page from a twentieth-century catalogue showing typical 'Japan' patterns re-issued by the King Street factory.

274 A page from a twentieth-century catalogue showing some of the earlier Derby figure-models re-issued by the King Street factory. Such pieces will bear the amended later mark, but without the word 'England' generally added to post-1891 wares.

Derby-Royal Crown Derby

ROYAL CROWN DERBY
(1876–present day)

The Royal Crown Derby Porcelain Company (originally the Derby Crown Porcelain Co. Ltd) was established in Osmaston Road, Derby, in 1876; but, contrary to general opinion, it had no direct connection with the original Derby works in Nottingham Road. The new company was founded by Edward Phillips formerly of the Royal Worcester Company, and by 1878 the new factory was in production. Initially earthenwares termed 'Crown Ware' were made, as well as porcelain.

The new Derby porcelain was often richly decorated in the old 'Japan' styles with rich gilding. The new shapes of the late Victorian era are shown in the contemporary photograph reproduced as Plate 275. Some fine figures and groups were made, including some copies of old Derby models such as the famous Mansion House Dwarfs.

The Royal Crown Derby period correctly dates from January 1890 when the company was appointed Manufacturers of Porcelain to Her Majesty Queen Victoria, and from this period the standard printed mark was amended to include the words 'Royal Crown Derby'.

Of the many talented artists employed, mention should be made of A. Gregory; G. Landgraff; Désiré Leroy—a Sèvres-trained artist whose painting and gilding are of the highest quality (see Plate 278); James Rouse, senior (1802–88) (see Plates 276–77), and his son of the same name (see Plate 280).

Apart from the hand-painted, individual pieces, the company has produced a range of traditional Derby 'Japan' patterns in rich blue, red, and gold designs. While most examples are of table wares, there are some miniature 'cabinet pieces' of great charm; some typical examples are shown in Plate 281. The Royal Crown Derby Porcelain Co. Ltd continues to the present day, and there is an interesting works collection illustrating the various aspects of Derby ceramic art.

The reader is referred to *Royal Crown Derby* by John Twitchett and Betty Bailey (Third edition Antique Collectors' Club, 1988).

From 1882 onwards all Crown Derby porcelain can be dated, for a year-cypher appears under the trade-mark. The key to these cyphers is published in my *Victorian Porcelain* (Herbert Jenkins, London, 1961) and the *Encyclopaedia of British Pottery and Porcelain Marks* (Herbert Jenkins, London, 1966).

275 A selection of Royal Crown Derby porcelains of the 1899 period. The original illustration appeared in the trade journal *Pottery Gazette*.

276 A well-painted Crown
Derby plate, painted and
signed by James Rouse
(1802–88), a talented artist first
employed at the original factory
in the 1820s. Diameter 9¼
inches. *c.* 1887.

277 A turquoise-ground tray,
the centre painted and signed
by James Rouse, an artist who
used rather dry-looking
enamels. In later years his
painting tended to be rather
wooden. 11 × 7¾ inches. *c.* 1885.

278 A fine-quality blue-ground Royal Crown Derby vase, enamelled and gilt by Désiré Leroy, an artist who earlier worked for Mintons. Printed mark with year-cypher for 1898. $8\frac{1}{4}$ inches high.

279 Three Royal Crown Derby vases painted by Désiré Leroy. Reproduced from an advertisement in *The Connoisseur* magazine, 1906.

280 A pair of vases charmingly painted by James Rouse, junior. 6½ inches high. *c.* 1890–95.

281 A selection of Royal Crown Derby miniature or 'toy' pieces, made in the present century and bearing typical 'Japan' patterns. Printed marks with year-cyphers ranging from 1914 to 1921. Watering-can 3⅛ inches high.

Doulton-Burslem

DOULTON-BURSLEM
(1882–present day)

The name Doulton is normally associated with stonewares made at the firm's celebrated Lambeth works in London; however, fine-quality porcelains have been made at the firm's works at Nile Street, Burslem, in the Staffordshire Potteries since 1883.

Henry Doulton gathered together at the Burslem factory a team of the leading artists of the day to decorate his newly introduced bone-china wares. Painters from Coalport, Copelands, Mintons, and Worcester, as well as some Continental artists of international note, were engaged. These men were encouraged to sign their work, and soon this late-starter in the production of fine porcelain was rivalling all competitors. Allowing for the taste of the time, the Doulton porcelains are amongst the most noteworthy of the 1890–1910 period, and now after a period of neglect are beginning to get the respect they deserve.

Each article bears one of the standard printed marks as shown below:

Moving to more modern times, mention must be made of the popular and lengthy series of Doulton figures and groups, and of the introduction in 1960 of 'English Translucent China'—a relatively inexpensive body now used for table wares of simple, modern shapes. The success of this new body led to the discontinuation of earthenwares, and the firm's present title, 'Doulton Fine China Ltd', aptly describes the products.

The reader is referred to *Royal Doulton, 1815-1965* by Desmond Eyles (Hutchinson & Co., London, 1965), *The Doulton Burslem Wares* by Desmond Eyles (Barrie & Jenkins, London, 1980). There are also several books and price guides on Doulton figures etc.

282 A Royal Doulton porcelain
vase painted by G. White. 11
inches high. *c.* 1900–1910.

283 A typical flower-painted
Doulton plate decorated by
Edward Raby. Diameter $9\frac{1}{4}$
inches. *c.* 1904.

opposite page
284 A fine Royal Doulton
porcelain vase decorated in the
typical manner of Harry
Allen. Printed mark. 14 inches
high. *c.* 1910–14.

Girl in a Swing-Class

'GIRL IN A SWING'-CLASS PORCELAINS
(c. 1749–54)

This rare, mid-eighteenth-century class of porcelain (formerly linked with the Chelsea factory) takes its name from one of the first pieces discovered—the figure of a girl in a swing, shown here as Plate 285.

While no marked examples are known and, as yet, the factory-site has not been identified, it is believed that these wares (which in some cases emulate Chelsea models) were made in London during the period 1749–54. The body is very like the early triangle-period Chelsea porcelains, but has a relatively higher percentage of lead (about 17%). The modelling of the figure is quite different from Chelsea and almost wooden. The nose is angular and pointed, forming a straight line from the forehead. The legs and arms tend to be long and thin. These characteristic features are clearly seen in Plates 285, 288–89.

The identified products include a series of birds (Plate 287). These and other examples from this factory are often mounted on easily identifiable hexagonal, curved bases. The applied leaves and flowers (Plate 286) are peculiar to this short-lived factory and also occur on some figure models (Plate 285). These birds, like the figures, occur in both the white and the decorated state, although some of the now white examples may have originally been embellished with unfired pigment which has worn off. The fired enamel decoration in the form of flower-sprays on the bases of some figures and on related useful wares is often characteristic (Plates 287, 291). Gilding does not occur on these porcelains. The birds and figures were formed by the slip-casting method (see page 19).

While the best-known examples of the 'Girl in a Swing' porcelains are figures, recent research has shown clearly that the factory (which must have been quite small) also produced other wares. We have, for example, a range of 'toys'—that is, scent-bottles, patch-boxes, seals, and the like, often with metal mounts. The undersides of the bases are often painted with a pink rose, and some other examples have a marbled effect. The jug and covered bowl shown in Plates 290–91 are of typical paste and glaze and bear flower-painting of a type found on the character-istic figures and bird models. Their comparatively recent discovery raises questions about other 'Girl in a Swing'-type functional porcelains. No doubt tea-services at least were made, and surviving pieces are awaiting identification.

I have purposely separated the discussion of these porcelains from the Chelsea section, where in other works, it is normally placed, in order to underline the present opinion that the wares originate from an entirely separate factory. As yet,

Colour Plate V A superbly gilt Derby scenic-painted vase, similar to the earlier Chelsea-Derby example shown in Plate 148. Crowned 'D' mark with crossed batons in red enamel. 13¾ inches high. *c.* 1815.

no firm facts are available, but it is believed that a group of Staffordshire workmen came to London in about 1747 to work at the Chelsea factory, but becoming dissatisfied, set up a rival works. Charles Gouyn, a jeweller who had formerly been associated with the Chelsea works, is thought to have been the spirit behind the new venture, and from at least May 1749, the main Chelsea factory disclaimed association with the 'Chelsea China Warehouse', the manager of which reported that his goods were supplied by Mr Charles Gouyn.

At the present time, probably less than a hundred examples of 'Girl in a Swing'-class porcelains are known to collectors, and examples are eagerly sought after and expensive. In fact, of all the British porcelains featured in this book, these rare London porcelains tend to be the most costly, notwithstanding their rather plain and stiff appearance. It is curious that we also know less about these wares than about any other variety. They lack a place-name, or even a personal association, although one day, the term 'Gouyn's porcelain' may be applied. While several learned ceramic scholars have contributed to our present knowledge, the best and most complete summary is contained in a paper by the late Arthur Lane and R. J. Charleston, published in the *Transactions of the English Ceramic Circle*, Vol. 5, Part 3 (1962). The reader is also referred to Mrs Adams' book *Chelsea Porcelain* (Barrie & Jenkins, London, 1987, chapter 5 and to G. Godden's *Encyclopaedia of British Porcelain Manufacturers* (Barrie & Jenkins, London, 1988).

285 The white figure from
which this class of mid-
eighteenth-century porcelain
derived its name. *c.* 1750.
6¼ inches high.

286 A detail from the bird model shown opposite, illustrating the characteristic flowers and leaves.

287 A typical 'girl in a swing' class bird. Note the shape of base and the style of bird-painting, also the large-size flowers (see opposite). *c.* 1750. $5\frac{1}{4}$ inches high.

288 A typical pair of 'girl in a swing'-class porcelain figures, displaying rather primitive modelling. These models also appear with enamelled decoration. 5¾ inches high. *c.* 1750.

289 & A A fine pair of 'girl in a swing'-class candlestick-figures; the long, straight noses are typical. These rare models also occur with enamelled decoration. 8 inches high.

290 A rare 'girl in a swing'-class creamer. Few useful wares from this factory have as yet been identified. 3¼ inches high.

291 A charming 'girl in a swing'-class sugar-bowl and cover, showing typical flower-painting. 5¼ inches high. This example is in the Victoria and Albert Museum.

245

Goss

GOSS
(c. 1858–1940)

William Henry Goss (1833–1906), after a period at the Copeland factory, established a small pottery at Stoke-on-Trent, and by the time of the 1862 Exhibition the Goss wares had won acclaim.

The early Goss wares are often of very good quality and some fine Parian figures and busts were made. A speciality of the works was jewelled Parian, the 'jewels' being set into the body. The pre-1880 Goss wares are often surprisingly finely potted and in many cases there is a similarity to the Belleek porcelains.

Glazed Parian ornaments of small size bearing reproductions of the Arms of various towns and cities were introduced by the Goss firm probably in the late 1880s, but the main period of this typical and well-known Goss ware was 1900–1920, during which time tens of thousands of inexpensive mementoes were produced. Typical specimens are shown in Plate 293. These are hardly high art but they fulfilled a demand, and the collection of Goss wares became a craze almost rivalling the postcard-collecting craze of the early 1900s. A quite large export trade was built up, largely destroyed by the 1914–18 war. The Goss cottages and houses are well modelled, and the collection of these and other Goss wares has recently experienced a revival. Books about these relatively modern wares include *A Pictorial Encyclopaedia of Goss China* by Diana Rees and Marjorie G. Cawley (The Ceramic Book Company, Newport, Mon., 1970) and *A Handbook of Goss China* by John Galpin. There are also numerous price guides published by the specialist dealer N. J. Pine, such as his *Price Guide to Goss China* (Milestone Publications, 1986).

In 1929 the Goss Company passed into the ownership of Cauldon Potteries Ltd, but the old association was retained by the use of the trading titles 'W. H. Goss Ltd' (1930–34) and 'Goss China Company Ltd' (1934–40). The production of Goss china ceased in 1940. It should be noted that several other firms made heraldic wares in the Goss Style. The Goss printed trade-mark is reproduced.

W. H. GOSS.

292 A three-handled Goss cup, having a relief-moulded portrait of W. H. Goss. The other sides show the arms of Stoke-on-Trent and the Goss trade-mark. 4½ inches high. *c.* 1900.

following page
293 A selection of typical Goss armorial mementoes such as were sold in most English towns in the first quarter of the present century. Printed crest trade-mark. All pieces under 3 inches high.

Grainger-Worcester

GRAINGER-WORCESTER
(*c.* 1801–1902)

As yet little research has been carried out on this branch of Worcester porcelain, and marked specimens of the pre-1830 period are scarce.

Thomas Grainger, who had been employed at the Chamberlain factory at Worcester and perhaps before that at the so-called Dr Wall Worcester works, established his own factory in St Martin's Street, Worcester in 1801. He then had as a partner the talented painter John Wood. It would appear at first that Grainger and Wood started purely as decorators of porcelain purchased in the white, but by about 1805 new shapes which we can recognise as Grainger appeared. Some bear painted trade-marks such as 'Grainger, Wood & Co.', 'Grainger, Wood', 'Grainger & Co.', or simple 'New China Works'. These relate to the 1801–12 period. With tea wares the Grainger workmen followed the Chamberlain practice of placing the mark *inside* the covers of teapots or sugar-bowls. Plates 294–96 show wares of this period.

In the 1812–39 period we find the partnership of Grainger, Lee & Co. at the New China Works at Worcester. Typical marked products are shown in Plates 297–98, but many examples, particularly of the useful wares, appear to have been issued without a factory-mark.

On Thomas Grainger's death in 1839 his son George succeeded him, under the new style 'George Grainger (& Co.)'. Most marks from this time on are clear and self-explanatory but others comprise only the initials G.W., G.G.W., G.G.& Co., or G. & Co. The initials S.P. or the words 'Semi Porcelain' can occur with these marks. This description relates to a hard, durable body introduced in 1848, and much used for dinner and dessert services. It has the appearance of a thickly potted porcelain (Plate 303), but it should really be classed as an earthenware.

Fine Parian wares were produced by George Grainger from the late 1840s, and from the 1860s a class of tinted Parian was made with an openwork design, which is sometimes gilded and of very fine workmanship. Some late Grainger porcelain is very similar to Royal Worcester wares of the 1880–1900 period, with misty landscape patterns, or birds, flowers, and animals in a subdued water-colour-like effect, and some attractive pâte-sur-pâte designs were also produced. In 1889 the Grainger firm was taken over by the famous Royal Worcester Company, although the Grainger works continued, using its own marks until 1902. Some of the basic printed marks are reproduced on the following page.

c. 1850–70   c. 1870–89   c. 1889–1902

The Grainger pattern-numbers found on useful wares are of various types. The early numbers to about the year 1839 were of simple form, progressing to 2019. From 1839 to 1845 a cross was added after the last digit, while in 1845 a new system of fractional numbers was started, expressed under the number 2. Later, in the Victorian era, the letter G was used as a prefix.

For further information on these interesting porcelains the reader is referred to H. & J. Sandon's specialist work *Grainger Worcester Porcelain* (Barrie & Jenkins, London, 1989).

294 A typical blue and gold Grainger-Worcester teapot, very similar to Chamberlain examples but note handle- and knob-forms. Written mark 'Grainger & Co. Worcester' inside cover. 5½ inches high. *c.* 1805.

295 A Grainger-Worcester sugar-boat and teacup, showing the Chamberlain-like shapes and style of decoration. Note especially the knob-form. Painted mark inside cover 'Grainger Wood & Co. Worcester. Warranted, 232.' *c.* 1805–10.

opposite page
296 Representative pieces from a Grainger-Worcester tea service, showing a version of the popular 'Japan' pattern found on contemporary Chamberlain and other wares. Written mark 'Grainger & Co. Worcester. Warranted. No. 140' inside cover. Creamer 4½ inches high. *c.* 1805–10.

297 A Grainger Lee & Co. 'Japan'-pattern dessert comport and dish. Comport 7¼ inches high. Painted name-mark. *c.* 1815–20.

298 Representative pieces from a superb blue-ground Grainger Lee & Co. dessert service, painted with named views. Comport 8 inches high. *c.* 1820–30.

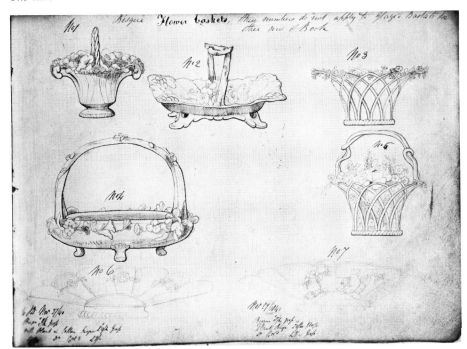

299 A page from the Grainger factory design-book, showing typical products which were made in bisque (unglazed) porcelain. This page is dated 27 November 1840.

300 A page from the Grainger factory design-book, showing animal models. Similar examples were made at Chamberlains and at other factories. *c.* 1840.

opposite page
301 Representative pieces from a Grainger blue-ground tea service of the type very often attributed to the Rockingham factory. Pattern-number 1847 + . Teapot 6½ inches high. *c.* 1835–45.

302 A blue-bordered Grainger dessert dish, the centre painted by the Swansea-trained artist David Evans. 9¼ inches long. *c.* 1840.

303 A Grainger-Worcester semi-porcelain plate bearing the impressed mark 'S.P. G.G.W.' (Semi Porcelain. George Grainger. Worcester). *c.* 1848–50.

304 A selection of Grainger's reticulated Parian wares as shown in the 1862 exhibition.

305 A typical Grainger reticulated vase bearing the shield mark of the 1870–89 period. 8¼ inches high.

306 A Grainger reticulated vase bearing the shield mark of the 1870–89 period. 6½ inches high.

257

Herculaneum-Liverpool

HERCULANEUM-LIVERPOOL
(*c.* 1796–1840)

The Herculaneum factory at Liverpool was established by Samuel Worthington in December 1796, most of the workmen being brought from the Staffordshire Potteries. At first Messrs Samuel Worthington & Co. produced only earthenwares and stonewares (see the companion volume) and on account of their location at this important port a large export trade was soon built up, mainly to North America.

The new factory was somewhat grandly titled the 'Herculaneum Pottery' and traded as the 'Herculaneum Pottery Company', the standard mark being simply the word 'Herculaneum', impressed—although most examples were not marked in any way.

Porcelain was probably introduced in about 1800; the early examples are of a decided cottagy appearance (the teapot shown in Plate 307 is a good example of this type), but soon rather more sophisticated patterns were produced, mainly in tea wares. The Empire-style vases (Plate 310) are the most accomplished products so far identified, but the research into Herculaneum porcelains is in its infancy. Its progress is limited by the small number of marked or otherwise documentary examples which are known.

The available facts on the whole range of Herculaneum wares are admirably presented in Alan Smith's *Illustrated Guide to Liverpool Herculaneum Pottery* (Barrie & Jenkins, London, 1970). The pattern-numbers are of a simple progressive type, without prefix. The series probably did not exceed a thousand.

307 An early Herculaneum-Liverpool porcelain teapot decorated in the New Hall manner. Note especially the handle- and knob-forms. Pattern-number 189. 6½ inches high. *c.* 1800–1805.

308 A fine Herculaneum-Liverpool scenic-painted teapot matching the pieces shown (in Plate 309). Impressed mark 'Herculaneum' on foot-rim. Length 10 inches. *c.* 1805–10.

309 Representative pieces from
a rare Herculaneum-Liverpool
porcelain tea set, showing with
the teapot (Plate 308)
characteristic shapes. Several
other factories issued similar
painted landscape-patterns.
c. 1805–10.

310 A Herculaneum-Liverpool
porcelain Empire-style vase
with apple-green ground.
Several English and Continental
firms produced vases of similar
forms, but this bears the printed
'Herculaneum Liverpool' mark
with bird-crest. 9⅝ inches high.
c. 1810–20.

Liverpool

The busy English West Coast port of Liverpool was, in the eighteenth century, one of the great centres of the English ceramic industry, having several small potteries, producing mainly tin-glazed Delft-type wares, but some manufacturers made translucent porcelain. In general, these eighteenth-century Liverpool porcelains were of a useful, rather than an ornamental, nature. These wares did not bear any distinguishing factory-mark or pattern-number. At their best they rival Worcester; at worst they were inexpensive, rather inferior copies of other porcelains, but they represent an interesting field of study, especially for the collector who has to confine his purchases to the less costly specimens.

Our present-day—still incomplete—knowledge of the various makes of Liverpool porcelain is largely due to the researches of one man, Dr Bernard Watney, and any review of these porcelains must draw largely on his published writing, which I detail later. It must be remembered, however, that in several instances we have no firm evidence to prove that our identification of these unmarked porcelains is correct, although the apparent period of a class fits well into the known period of a manufacturer's working life.

There is no one type of Liverpool porcelain; each group must be considered separately and these different classes are here briefly featured in chronological order.

RICHARD CHAFFERS & CO.
(*c*. 1754–65)

This Company was established at Liverpool, on Shaw's Brow, by at least 1747. Soapstone-type porcelain was being made by about 1756, when Richard Chaffers went to Cornwall to negotiate for the all-important soap rock, but possibly before this date the Chaffers' porcelain contained bone ash. Normally both blue and white and enamelled pieces bear designs showing the prevailing Oriental taste. The jugs shown in Plates 311 and 312 are typical. Richard Chaffers died in 1765 and his factory was continued by Philip Christian & Co.

SAMUEL GILBODY
(*c.* 1754–61)

This young potter took over his father's earthenware pottery at Shaw's Brow in about 1754, when he was not yet twenty-one. In 1758 he was advertising 'China ware of all sorts, equal for service and beauty to any made in England'. These porcelains probably date from about 1754. The quality and charm of some of the Gilbody enamelled porcelain is illustrated in Plate 313, while Plate 314 shows one of Gilbody's porcelain figures, among the very few which were produced at Liverpool. This specimen links with excavated 'wasters' from the factory-site. (See a paper by Alan Smith, 'Samuel Gilbody, Some Recent Finds at Liverpool', published in the *Transactions of the English Ceramic Circle*, Vol. 7, Part 2, 1969.) An enamelled figure of Minerva is currently on display at the Victoria and Albert Museum, and other models may well await discovery.

WILLIAM BALL
(*c.* 1755–69)

The porcelains previously attributed to this Liverpool potter are now, as a result of excavations at Vauxhall in London, believed to have been made by John Sanders in partnership with Nicholas Crisp, in the period 1753-1764. The body, and little furrows are quite common.

WILLIAM REID & CO.
(*c.* 1755–61)

The porcelains formerly attributed to William Reid, as Plate 319 are now believed to have been produced by Joseph Wilson at Limehouse, London, *c.* 1747–8 or slightly later at Newcastle-under-Lyme, Staffordshire.

PHILIP CHRISTIAN & CO.
(c. 1765–76)

Philip Christian continued Chaffers' factory at Shaw's Brow, where he made soap-stone-type porcelains. The coffee pot (Plate 320) is a good example of this class and the hand of the flower-painter is to be seen on many other specimens. The under-glaze-blue pieces are painted with fine strokes, and much use is made of a mass of small dots; the blue tends to be slightly grey and rather pale.

PENNINGTON & PART
(c. 1770–99)

There were several Pennington brothers potting in Liverpool in the eighteenth century. One, Seth, was in partnership with John Part, and the bone-ash porcelains shown in Plates 321–23 are believed to have been made by this partnership. The later wares of the 1760s often bear rather poor underglaze-blue prints, and in form and general quality the Fisherman-subject coffee pot (Plate 323) does not seriously rival the Caughley or Worcester pieces bearing the same design. The glaze is often slightly blued and speckled. Apart from the blue-decorated pieces, enamelled decoration occurs normally in rather simple designs (Plate 324).

THOMAS WOLFE & CO.
(c. 1795–1800)

Porcelains bearing overglaze prints such as that depicted in Plate 325 have been attributed to this firm at the Islington Pottery, but they seem to the present writer to be of an earlier period, although their Liverpool origin is not disputed. The factory 'wasters' shown in Plates 326–27 bear underglaze-blue prints and were excavated from the 'Islington China Manufactory' site. An advertisement issued in June 1800 shows that Wolfe's partners were Miles Mason (see page 295) and John Luckcock, and that the firm was then about to be closed. These porcelains appear to be of a type of hard-paste porcelain.

For the later Herculaneum Liverpool porcelain the reader is referred to page 258.

Very good accounts of the various Liverpool manufacturers and their porcelains are contained in: *English Blue and White Porcelain of the 18th Century* by B. Watney (Faber & Faber, London, 1973) and Maurice Hillis' paper 'The Liverpool Porcelains' published as an occasional paper by the Northern Ceramic Society in 1985.

Various specialist papers are published in the following *Transactions of the English Ceramic Circle*: 'Liverpool Porcelain' by T. Knowles Boney, Vol. 4, Part 1, 1957; 'Four Groups of Porcelain, possibly Liverpool' by B. Watney, Vol. 4, Part 5, 1959; 'Four Groups of Porcelain, possibly Liverpool' by B. Watney, Vol. 5, Part 1, 1960; 'The Porcelain of Chaffers, Christian and Pennington' by B. Watney, Vol. 5, Part 5, 1964; 'John Baddeley of Shelton' by John Mallet, Vol. 6, Part 3, 1967; 'Samuel Gilbody . . .' by Alan Smith, Vol. 7, Part 2, 1969.

Colour Plate VI A Lowestoft soft-paste porcelain teapot, cover and stand of a rare late form. The simple enamelled decoration is typical of this factory's products of the 1790s. The enamelled Lowestoft porcelains do not bear a factory mark. 6 inches high. *c.* 1795.

311 A Liverpool porcelain jug
from the Chaffers' factory,
painted in underglaze-blue.
10¾ inches high. *c.* 1760.

312 A fluted Liverpool jug
from the Chaffers' factory,
painted in underglaze-blue.
8¼ inches high. *c.* 1760.

313 A most attractive Liverpool
tankard from the Gilbody
factory, painted in enamel
colours. 5 inches high.
c. 1754–61.

314 A very rare Gilbody
Liverpool porcelain figure,
recently identified with the
help of matching 'wasters'
found near the factory-site.
c. 1754–61.

315 A most attractive blue and white saucer painted in a bright blue under a soft, warm, almost oily, glaze. Diameter 7¼ inches. This type of porcelain is now attributed to Sanders and Crisp at Vauxhall *c.* 1753-1764.

316 A Vauxhall porcelain bowl and creamer painted in a typical bright underglaze-blue, with Chinese-style motifs. Creamer 3 inches high *c.* 1753-64.

317 A rare Vauxhall porcelain sauce-boat enamelled in the Chelsea red-anchor style. 8¼ inches long. *c.* 1753-64.

318 A Vauxhall tea bowl and saucer decorated in underglaze-blue with overglaze enamels and gilding. Bearing the owner's initials and the date, 1764. This is perhaps part of a marriage service.

319 A selection of pieces formerly attributed to William Reid's factory at Liverpool. Finds on the Limehouse site in London early in 1990 suggest that these porcelains were made by Joseph Wilson at Limehouse, or later when he moved to Newcastle-under-Lyme, Staffordshire. Teapot 4¾ inches high, *c.* 1747–8.

320 A finely designed, Liverpool porcelain coffee pot from the Christian factory, enamelled by a hand found on much Christian porcelain. Note the graceful handle and moulded spout-feature that lift this example above the general level of Liverpool wares. 10 inches high. *c.* 1765–70.

321 A Liverpool porcelain tea bowl and saucer painted in underglaze-blue. This is rather a poor, inexpensive example made by the Penningtons. *c.* 1775–80.

322 A Pennington-Liverpool tea bowl and saucer printed in underglaze-blue with a rather crudely engraved design, somewhat typical of these wares. *c.* 1775–85.

271

opposite page
323 A Pennington-Liverpool coffee pot bearing a rather poor copy of the Caughley and Worcester 'Fisherman' design (see Plates 76–78, 89, 91 and 534). The handle- and spout-forms are uninspired and point to a Liverpool origin in the 1770–80 period. The glaze is blued and speckled. 8½ inches high.

324 An inscribed and dated Pennington-Liverpool teapot painted in overglaze enamels. 7 inches high. 1790.

325 A moulded Liverpool creamer of unusual form decorated in underglaze blue. From one of the Pennington factories *c.* 1780–5. 4½ inches high.

326 Unglazed fragments of blue-printed porcelains found at Liverpool on the site of the Thomas Wolfe & Co. factory—these porcelains do not seem to relate to the overglaze-printed examples attributed to this factory (see Plate 325). *c.* 1795–1800.

327 A blue-printed Liverpool tea bowl and saucer shown with a matching unglazed 'waster'. The body is rather hard-looking and is attributed to Thomas Wolfe & Co., a partnership between Wolfe, Miles Mason, and John Luckcock which was dissolved in June 1800.

Longton Hall

LONGTON HALL
(*c.* 1750–60)

This short-lived factory is famous because it was thought to be the first in the Staffordshire Potteries to make porcelain, rather than the traditional earthenwares, and although the wares are often thickly potted and clumsy, the surviving specimens are eagerly sought after.

It is to Dr Bernard Watney that we are indebted for our present-day knowledge of the history and products of this relatively small factory, and all collectors should study his excellent book *Longton Hall Porcelain* (Faber & Faber, London, 1957). The potter William Littler is normally associated with this factory, but he had two now little-known partners, William Nicklin and William Jenkinson. This latter partner had apparently discovered the art of making porcelain and had established a factory by 1751, but by mid-1753 he had sold his shares to Nathaniel Firmin. In 1755, when the partners were in financial difficulty, Robert Charlesworth joined the concern, infusing new capital. However, in May 1760 Charlesworth dissolved the partnership; the factory closed, and much of the finished goods were sold at auction in Salisbury.

The Longton Hall porcelains included the standard underglaze-blue wares made in the style of the popular Oriental porcelains, though the wares most characteristic of this Staffordshire pottery are the often rather clumsy-looking leaf-shaped table wares (Plates 330–32). Other characteristic pieces are decorated with a rich, streaky blue—very prone to running in the glaze (Plate 335). This is traditionally referred to as 'Littler's blue'. A useful pointer to a Longton Hall attribution is the dark 'scum-line' very often seen where the glaze ends. Figures and rare groups were made; these are of rather heavy weight, with somewhat clumsily finished bases. The cheeks often have the pigment stippled on.

Most Longton Hall porcelain is unmarked. Certain small signs, numerals, and chemical signs can occur, both on enamelled specimens and on wares decorated in underglaze-blue, but the generally accepted factory-mark is reproduced right. In the past this was regarded as representing crossed L's for Littler-Longton, but the device may well represent the initials J and L, for Jenkinson-Littler or Jenkinson-Longton. Although given as a factory-mark, it was, in fact, quite rarely used, and most specimens are unmarked.

After the closure of the Longton Hall factory in Staffordshire, William Littler went to West Pans, near Musselburgh, where he decorated old Longton blanks until at least 1777. Some rare blue-glazed earthenware apparently made from old Longton

Hall moulds may have been made at West Pans, but research continues on this later aspect of Littler's productions.

The reader is referred to: *Longton Hall Porcelain* by B. Watney (Faber & Faber, London, 1957) and *British Porcelain 1745–1850*, edited by R. J. Charleston, Longton Hall chapter by B. Watney (E. Benn, London, 1965).

Details on the West Pans venture are given in a paper by the late Arthur Lane, published in the *Transactions of the English Ceramic Circle*, Vol. 5, Part 2, 1961. Also a joint-paper by Mavis Bimson, John Ainslie, and B. Watney, published in the *Transactions*, Vol. 6, Part 2, 1966.

I have, in the first line, written in the past tense as recent research has indicated that porcelain was being made in Staffordshire at Newcastle-under-Lyme in the mid-1740s. For the present state of this research the reader is referred to a paper by Paul Bemrose published in the *Transactions of the English Ceramic Circle*, Vol. 9, Part 1, 1973.

328 A small-sized Longton-Hall teapot decorated in underglaze-blue. Note the handle-form. 4 inches high. *c.* 1755.

329 A relief-moulded Longton Hall teapot painted in underglaze-blue. Shown with matching 'wasters' from the factory-site. 5½ inches high. *c.* 1750–60.

330 A typical Longton Hall leaf-shaped sauce-boat. 4¾ inches long. *c.* 1750–60.

331 Three typical Longton Hall leaf-shaped wares. The enamelled view with castle-like tower is characteristic. Diameter of larger dish 8¾ inches. *c.* 1755.

278

332 A rare, but typically
Longton Hall, pair of leaf-
shaped double-handled sauce-
boats. 8 inches long. *c.* 1750–60.

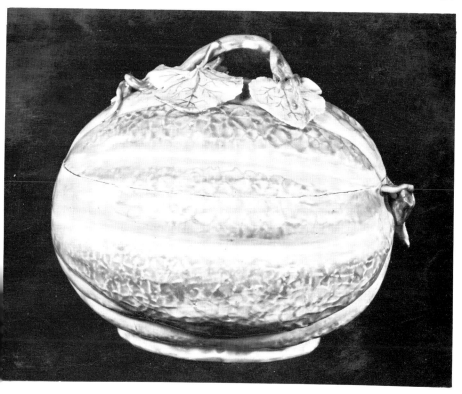

333 A rare Longton Hall
covered dessert-box in fruit
form. Several related shapes
were made. 6½ inches long.
c. 1750–60.

279

334 A rare Longton Hall basket of flowers made in two pieces to form a tureen or box. 7¾ inches high. *c.* 1755–60.

335 Two Longton Hall plates of typical shape, the borders painted in underglaze-blue—a colour very prone to run, as demonstrated by the centre vase. Vase 11¾ inches high. *c.* 1750–60.

336 A fine set of three Longton Hall covered vases painted in a style found on many specimens. 8½ and 10¾ inches high. *c.* 1755.

337 Three Longton Hall specimens. Note especially the relief-moulded border to the plate and the characteristic handle to the tankard. Diameter of plate 7⅝ inches. *c.* 1755–60.

338 A Longton Hall figure of
a goatherd. The typical streaky
underglaze-blue occurs on the
cloak. 9¾ high. *c.* 1755.

339 A small Longton Hall
figure on a typical base. 5¼
inches high. *c.* 1755.

340 A Longton Hall jug of a characteristic shape, one found with various styles of decoration. 7½ inches high. *c.* 1755.

Lowestoft

LOWESTOFT
(1757–99)

The Lowestoft porcelain is a soft-paste body with some 40% of bone ash, and in both chemical make-up and appearance it is very similar to the Bow porcelains. Lowestoft in Suffolk (then a fishing village) is on the extreme East Coast of England, remote from the main centres of the ceramic industry and from the large cities. Consequently, the Lowestoft porcelains were made primarily for the local markets. Many special commissions were undertaken, and there is a documentary sequence of dated and inscribed pieces, among them the mug shown in Plate 346.

Most Lowestoft porcelain is in the form of useful table wares, the tea wares outnumbering all other objects, and from 1757 to the early 1770s all the decoration was in underglaze-blue. A feature of the early wares is the attractive relief-moulded design (see Plates 341–45). The placing of the painter's number on the inside of the foot-rim is also a useful guide (Plate 342) as is the flat-glazed base of many stands (Plate 348) or tea caddies.

In general, the Lowestoft designs have a naïve charm, being very broadly based on Chinese porcelains. A class of porcelain made in the 1770s follows the Oriental fashion for underglaze-blue in conjunction with overglaze enamels—reds, greens, and some slight gilding. Some enamelled wares of the 1780s closely follow the Chinese figure- and flower-painted export wares imported by the English East India Company (Colour Plate VI and Plates 351 and 354). Rarer types of Lowestoft porcelain show naturalistic flower-painting (Plate 350) or English views. In the 1790s French taste is reflected in simple sprig patterns and attractive gilt designs— the soft English porcelain giving an almost toy-like quality to the piece (Plate 349). Apart from the individual, inscribed pieces (Plate 346) the rarest classes of Lowestoft porcelain comprise certain figures, two pairs of which are shown in Plates 352–53, of which the bases and the type of thick applied leaves are characteristic, as is the manner in which the back of the supporting tree-trunk is enamelled. The bases of this rare class of figures are flat and glazed over. Some small circular plaques or 'birth-tablets' seem unique to this factory, underlining the personal nature of the factory's output, as they record the name and date of birth of local children.

While it was formerly believed that the Lowestoft factory continued into the nineteenth century, recent research suggests that it closed in 1799. Certainly some of its leading factory people were being employed in Worcester at this period.

A very full range of Lowestoft porcelain, including many documentary inscribed pieces is featured in my *Lowestoft Porcelains* (Antique Collectors' Club, 1985), a book which enlarges on the points made in this brief summary.

The reader should bear in mind that Continental imitations of Lowestoft porcelain were made in the nineteenth century. These are of hard-paste porcelain, quite different from the relatively soft, friendly, Lowestoft body, but some fakes bear the name 'Lowestoft'. No pattern-numbers were employed and the enamelled pieces are devoid of any mark. Some copies of Dresden or Worcester patterns may bear the blue crossed-swords or crescent mark of these wares, but apart from the painter's personal numbers or other sign, no true Lowestoft factory-mark was employed.

The date of establishment of this factory is open to some doubt, on account of the discovery of an insurance policy dated 27 January 1756, listing 'Four warehouses with chambers over and a kilnhouse'. The situation is, however, complicated by mention in the same document of the 'stock of stone-ware' not porcelain, possibly also by the difference between the old style of calendar and the new. Under the old style, January 1756 would be 1757 by our present standard. See paper by Mrs Elizabeth Adams in the *Transactions of the English Ceramic Circle*, Vol. 9, Part 1, 1973.

Recent books on Lowestoft porcelains include *Lowestoft Porcelain* by Geoffrey Godden (revised edition, Antique Collectors' Club, 1985), *Early Lowestoft* by Christopher Spencer (Ainsworth & Nelson, 1981) and Sheenah Smith's two-volume study *Lowestoft Porcelain in Norwich Castle Museum*.

341 A selection of early
Lowestoft soft-paste porcelains,
relief-moulded in the manner of
James Hughes and painted in
the Chinese style in underglaze-
blue. Like other Lowestoft
porcelains these pieces bear a
painter's number inside the
foot-rim (see Plate 342). Sauce-
boat 8 inches high. *c.* 1760–65.

342 A pair of relief-moulded Lowestoft sauce-boats, showing the typical placing of the painter's number, also the blue dashes each side of the handle-junction. $5\frac{1}{2}$ inches long. *c.* 1765.

343 A relief-moulded Lowestoft teapot of a typical type. Note especially the key-like underglaze-blue border. The modeller's initials IH appear under the central panel (arrow). These initials for James Hughes appear also on related wares. 6 inches high. *c.* 1761.

344 A documentary, inscribed Lowestoft sauce-boat, illustrating a characteristic relief-moulded design. Painter's number 5. 7½ inches long. Dated 1770.·

345 A typical Lowestoft relief-moulded sauce-boat, the decoration being *printed* in underglaze-blue, in places, washed over by hand. 8¼ inches high. *c.* 1775.

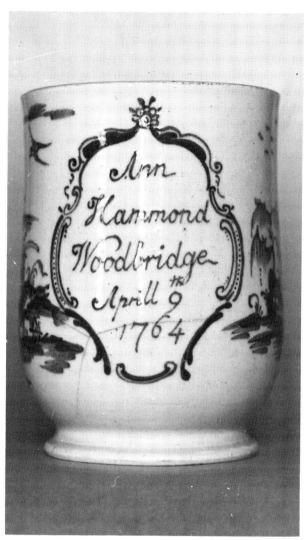

346 A typical, but rare, inscribed Lowestoft tankard painted in underglaze-blue. Many such pieces were made to individual order. Painter's number 3 inside foot-rim. $4\frac{2}{3}$ inches high.

347 A back-view of a Lowestoft blue and white jug, showing a typical handle and the characteristic blue dashes by the handle-joint. Painter's mark 6. $5\frac{3}{4}$ inches high. *c.* 1760–65.

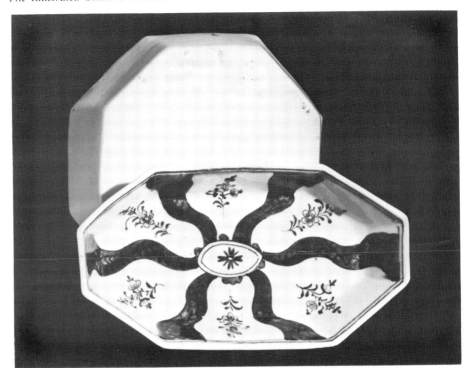

348 The reverse of a Lowestoft teapot-stand of typical form, showing the characteristic, flat, glazed-over base, the front of a matching spoon-tray, of the 'Robert Browne' pattern. Tray $6\frac{1}{4} \times 3\frac{2}{3}$ inches. *c.* 1775–80.

349 A Lowestoft saucer and tea caddy decorated in underglaze-blue, illustrating the naïve, child-like quality of some of the standard Chinese-style designs. Caddy $3\frac{9}{10}$ inches high. *c.* 1785–90.

350 A fine Lowestoft coffee pot painted in enamel colours by the 'Tulip painter' in his typical manner. $8\frac{1}{4}$ inches high. *c.* 1775.

351 A Lowestoft jug of typical form enamelled in the Oriental style on a brick-red ground. $8\frac{1}{4}$ inches high. *c.* 1776.

352 A rare pair of Lowestoft *putti*, the bases of characteristic form, with the thick leaves found on other Lowestoft porcelains. 5¼ inches high. *c.* 1780–85.

353 A very rare pair of Lowestoft musicians (the man's triangle and the woman's lute-like instrument are missing). The decoration, the flowers and leaves, and the decorated back-support are characteristic. Flat, glazed-over bases. 6¾ and 7 inches high. *c.* 1780.

354 A typical Lowestoft sparrow-beak creamer enamelled in a characteristic manner. Such creamers of this standard shape appear with various stock-patterns. $3\frac{1}{2}$ inches high. *c.* 1780–85.

355 An enamelled Lowestoft tea bowl and saucer enamelled in a simple but attractive design. These Lowestoft enamels are rather wet-looking —see Colour Plate VI. *c.* 1790.

356 A Lowestoft tea bowl and saucer of a rare shape, decorated in a charming, simple style in gold. Diameter of saucer 5 inches. *c.* 1790–95.

357 A selection of rare Lowestoft 'Trifles' enamelled in typical styles and bearing the place-names of Lowestoft and nearby towns. A further example is shown as Colour Plate VII in the *Illustrated Guide to Lowestoft Porcelain* (Herbert Jenkins, London, 1969). Pounce-pot (sander) 2½ inches high. *c.* 1790–99. *N.B.* These 'Trifle' pieces have been reproduced—mainly in a Continental hard-paste body.

Masons

MASONS
(*c.* 1800–13)

The Mason name is usually associated with the heavy and durable 'Patent Ironstone China', which is really an earthenware, but Miles Mason had previously made good-quality porcelains, firstly in partnership at Liverpool (see page 264) and in Staffordshire, and by at least 1804 on his own account at Lane Delph in the Staffordshire Potteries.

Miles Mason was born in 1752 and had been a china-retailer in London before turning to the production of his own wares. His partnership with George Wolfe being dissolved in July 1800, Mason continued alone and introduced at his former earthenware manufactory the production of porcelain. His advertisement published in the *Morning Herald* on 15 October 1804 indicates Mason's former trade in Chinese porcelains and his subsequent endeavours to match these fashionable Chinese wares.

MASON'S CHINA

. . . Miles Mason, late of Fenchurch Street, London, having been a principal purchaser of Indian [a contemporary term for Chinese wares imported by the East India Company] porcelain till the prohibition of that article by heavy duties, has established a manufactory at Lane Delph, near Newcastle-under-Lime, upon the principle of the Indian [Chinese] and Seve [Sèvres] china.
. . . his article is warranted from the manufactory to possess superior qualities to Indian Nankin china, being more beautiful as well as more durable and not so liable to snip at the edges; more difficult to break. . . . N.B. The articles are stamped on the bottom of the large pieces to prevent imposition.

The mark found impressed is M Mason, and the key pieces illustrated here in Plates 358–61 bear this standard mark. The name is also found rarely incorporated in blue-printed marks (Plate 364). Many examples do not bear any name-mark, but the shapes shown are characteristic ones which should enable identification to be made. The porcelain body is the standard early nineteenth-century one, being little different from that employed by other manufacturers—the glaze is normally rather hard-looking but free of crazing. The Mason pattern-numbers are progressive of simple form, the numbers probably not exceeding six hundred.

The production of porcelain would seem to have taken second-place soon after 1813, when the exceedingly popular 'Masons Patent Ironstone China' was introduced (see the companion volume, *British Pottery: an Illustrated Guide*). For further illustrations of typical porcelains, see *Staffordshire Porcelain* (Granada, 1983), chapter 11.

358 The underside of a Mason porcelain creamer of the 1805–1810 period, showing impressed in the foot-rim the standard mark 'M Mason'. Painted pattern-number 84.

359 An early Miles Mason porcelain plate with tea bowl and saucer. Enamelled with a New Hall-style cottagy floral design—pattern-number 3. Plate with impressed mark 'M Mason'. Diameter $7\frac{7}{8}$ inches. *c.* 1800–1805.

360 Representative pieces from a Miles Mason porcelain tea set, illustrating typical shapes, decorated in this case with a Chinese-style pattern similar to that on the Chinese porcelains in which Masons had formerly dealt as a retailer in London. Teapot $10\frac{1}{2}$ inches long. *c.* 1805.

361 A Miles Mason porcelain covered sugar-box, the form linking with the shapes shown in Plate 360, but in this case decorated with an underglaze-blue printed design also relating to the popular Chinese porcelains. Note the characteristic knob-shape. Pattern-number 49, 5¼ inches high. *c.* 1805.

362 A gilt Miles Mason creamer of simple form. 4½ inches high. *c.* 1810.

363 Representative parts of a Miles Mason tea set of pattern-number 84. Noteworthy are the cup-handle forms, the creamer shape, and particularly the knob, which also occurs on related teapots. The underside of the marked creamer is shown in Plate 358. Creamer 4¾ inches high. *c.* 1810.

opposite page

364 Representative pieces from a Miles Mason tea set showing characteristic shapes (the teapot-form is, however, very similar to that from other factories) bearing an underglaze-blue printed design. Blue-printed Miles Mason mark with Chinese-style square design. Teapot 6¼ inches high. *c.* 1810–13.

365 Two, of a set of three, Miles Mason porcelain vases. This form with the prominent mask-head handles is unique to Masons. Impressed 'M Mason' mark. 6¼ and 8 inches high. *c.* 1810.

366 Three fine-quality Miles Mason porcelain vases, showing further characteristic shapes. Impressed 'M Mason' marks. Large vase 11½ inches high. *c.* 1810.

367 An impressed-marked
'M Mason' vase of rare form
with richly gilt borders. The
final to the cover is missing.
7 inches high. *c.* 1810.

Minton

MINTON
(*c.* 1793–present day)

Like other Staffordshire porcelain manufacturers, Thomas Minton began by making earthenware. The production of translucent bone china or porcelain dates from the later part of 1797. The earliest Minton porcelains, mainly tea wares, bear only a pattern-number, not a factory-mark, and the designs were quite simple and attractive. The factory pattern-book shows that some so-called New Hall cottage, floral designs were produced. Plates 368–70 illustrate the early unmarked Minton porcelains, matching the factory pattern-book.

By about 1805 this Stoke firm employed the following enamelled mark, having a similarity to the well-known Sèvres factory-mark. The Minton pattern-number was normally added below this device, as in the example shown, although sometimes only the letter M appears.

These marks were used until about 1816, when the production of porcelain ceased, to be commenced again in 1824. By 1816 the Minton pattern-numbers had reached approximately one thousand, but today these Minton porcelains of the 1797–1816 period are quite rare. In shape, pattern, and quality they are very close to the better-known Spode porcelains, although the soft Minton glaze had a tendency to craze.

The second period of Minton porcelain started in 1824 and has continued to the present day. From this period the bone-china body became whiter and more compact and the potting became thinner. The shapes are more ambitious, showing relief-moulding and extensive use of ground colours (Plate 375). Superb tea and dessert services were made and richly decorated by talented artists, several of whom had been trained at the Derby factory.

Apart from useful table wares, a large range of ornamental wares was produced, including many vase-forms. From the mid-1830s much emphasis was placed on floral-encrusted decoration. Such pieces, in the Dresden style, very often bear a copy of the Dresden crossed-swords mark, and these porcelains are often incorrectly classed as Coalport or Coalbrookdale (see page 150). The Minton pattern-books prove their origin (see Plate 383 and the *Illustrated Encyclopaedia of British Pottery and Porcelain*). Apart from the crossed-swords-marked examples, the Minton ornamental porcelains of the 1830–50 period are unmarked, and until recently many specimens have been attributed to other factories—Derby, Rockingham, and even Swansea. Some of the Minton porcelains of this period were painted by the famous Derby fruit- and flower-painter Thomas Steel, an artist employed by Mintons from at least March 1832 (see Plates 379–81).

The Derby influence is also seen in the unmarked Minton porcelain figures. Many of these were introduced by former Derby modellers such as Edward and Samuel Keys. The Minton figures fall into two categories, the undecorated and unglazed 'bisque' examples showing superb workmanship and often lacy effects (Plates 386–389) and the glazed and richly enamelled specimens (Plates 390–92)—but each model can occur in either vastly different style. Before about 1845, the Minton figures and groups were unmarked and have recently been identified by the present writer with the help of the factory design-books. In a general work of this nature only a very few typical examples can be featured, but all the figure models and ornamental porcelains of the pre-1850 period are listed in my specialist work *Minton Pottery and Porcelain of the First Period, 1793–1850* (Herbert Jenkins, London, 1968). With reference to figures, it must be stated that the Minton firm was one of the earliest and foremost manufacturers of Parian figures and groups, a body introduced in the early 1840s (see page 361).

This brings us forward to the 1850–1900 period, a period dominated by Herbert Minton, who had succeeded his father, Thomas, on his early death in 1836. The prevailing ceramic taste was that of the French Sèvres factory, with its rich ground colours. Some Minton models were very closely copied from Sèvres originals, although the Minton marks and not faked Sèvres marks were used. The Minton firm was one of the leading firms of truly international repute and many French artists were employed at Minton's Stoke factory under the famous French Art Director, Leon Arnoux. The Continental artists and modellers included Antonin Boullemier, Carrier de Belleuse, Christian Henk, Louis Jahn, Emile Jeannest, Desire Leroy, William Mussill, Edouard Rischgitz, and Marc Louis Solon. For pure quality the porcelains produced at Minton's in the 1860–80 period would be hard to better, and certainly the cost of such workmanship today would be prohibitive. These Minton wares will probably bear one of the following basic printed marks:

c. 1850–60.   c. 1855–65.

c. 1863–72.   c. 1873–1912.   c. 1912–50.

Apart from the printed marks from 1862 to c. 1873, the impressed name-mark 'Minton' was used, and from c. 1873 onwards the plural form, 'Mintons'. In addition, year-cyphers were impressed, so that by reference to the books listed at the end of this section the exact year of manufacture can be discovered.

In addition to the fine Minton porcelains, this great firm produced a rich selection of earthenwares, including the 'Majolica' body, which it introduced to this country in 1850. The Minton factory to this day remains at Stoke, in the heart of the Staffordshire Potteries, continuing the tradition for fine English bone china, a tradition built up from the time Thomas Minton first started to produce this body in the closing years of the eighteenth century.

For further details of Minton porcelains the reader is referred to *Minton Pottery and Porcelain of the First Period 1793–1850* by G. A. Godden (Herbert Jenkins, London, 1968), *Victorian Porcelain* by G. A. Godden (Herbert Jenkins, London, 1961) and to chapter 9 of the general work *Staffordshire Porcelain* (Granada, 1983).

368 An early Minton porcelain teapot of characteristic form, bearing a naïvely painted Chinese-style enamel pattern. Marked only with the pattern-number 105, which agrees with the factory pattern-book. 6¼ inches high. *c.* 1800.

opposite page
369 Two attractive, early Minton porcelain mugs of a type often attributed to the Pinxton factory, which issued similar designs. The Minton pattern-number 58 is seen on the base of one; this agrees with the Minton pattern-book. 4½ inches high. *c.* 1800–1805.

370 Representative pieces from an early Minton porcelain tea service of pattern-number 72, illustrating characteristic forms of the 1800 period. The painted pattern-number is shown on one reversed saucer, and the related design from the factory pattern-book is reproduced. The preservation of these records has enabled much unmarked Minton porcelain to be identified and the shapes recorded. Teapot 10½ inches long. *c.* 1800.

opposite page
371 Representative pieces from a blue-ground Minton tea service bearing the painted crossed-L's mark with the pattern-number 560. Note that these are standard shapes employed—with minor amendments—at most factories of the 1805–10 period. Teapot 6¼ inches high.

372 A rare Minton inkstand, gilt on a rich blue ground, bearing the standard crossed-L's mark with the pattern-number 780. 6¾ inches long. *c.* 1812–16.

373 A set of three blue-ground vases of the popular 780 design —a pattern found also on tea wares and many Minton shapes. Painted crossed-L's mark with pattern-number. 6 and 6½ inches high. *c.* 1812.

opposite page

374 Representative pieces from a Minton blue-ground porcelain tea service, illustrating typical shapes of the 1812–14 period. However, quite similar forms—particularly of the cup—were standard at this period and were made at several factories with minor amendments. The painted crossed-L's mark is shown on the upturned cup. Pattern-number 876—one of the last for the first period of Minton porcelain. Teapot 5¾ inches high. *c.* 1815.

375 A fine and typical Minton porcelain dessert service of the second, or post-1825, period, with green borders and relief-moulded ornamentation. Marked with pattern-number 498. Centrepiece 7 inches high. *c.* 1825–30.

376 Representative pieces from a typical Minton porcelain relief-moulded tea set of the second, or post-1825, period. The quality of the porcelain, the potting, painting, and gilding, is superb. Pattern-number 702. Teapot 6 inches high. *c.* 1830–35.

377 An attractive Minton
Pembroke ewer, richly gilt on
a maroon ground, the
landscape-panel painted in the
typical style of the 1830s. $9\frac{1}{4}$
inches high.

378 A rare Minton 'night
lamp', shape-number 40 in the
factory design-book. For many
years this piece has been
thought to be of Swansea make,
a fact that reflects the quality
of these unmarked Minton
porcelains. $8\frac{1}{8}$ inches high.
c. 1830.

Colour Plate VII A Minton covered vase of the 'Octagon Chelsea' shape, design-number 165 in the factory shape-book. The flower-painting by J. Smith, landscape-panels on reverse side. $17\frac{1}{2}$ inches high (these vases and most other standard shapes were made in three or more different sizes). *c.* 1840–45.

379 A small-sized Minton urn-vase, richly gilt on a green ground. The floral panel painted by Thomas Steel, the former Derby and Rockingham artist. 5 inches high. *c.* 1832–35.

380 A blue-ground Minton urn-vase, the panel painted by Thomas Steel. The form of the recess under the base is typical —although these cut corners can occur on other wares. $7\frac{1}{2}$ inches high. *c.* 1832–35.

following page
381 Two, of a set of three, superb blue-ground Minton vases of the 'Wellington' shape, shape-number 11 in the factory design-book. The front panels are by the Derby-trained artist Thomas Steel. The smaller vase is reversed to show the fine and typical tooled gilding by Thomas Till. $13\frac{1}{4}$ and 15 inches high. *c.* 1832–35.

382 A floral-encrusted Minton 'Dresden scroll vase', design-number 76 in the factory design-book (the basic shape was also made without the flowers). Wares of this type were formerly attributed to the Coalport factory, but the Minton factory records prove their real origin. 12 inches high. *c.* 1835–40.

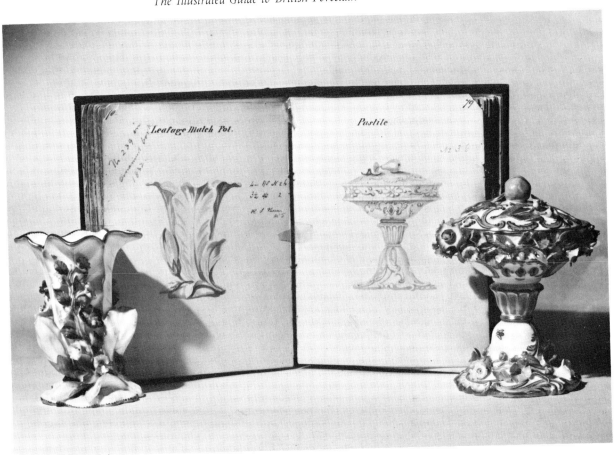

383 Two Minton floral-encrusted pieces shown with the factory shape-book, the drawings featuring the plain versions. 'Pastile' $5\frac{1}{4}$ inches high. *c.* 1835.

384 Three Minton 'Chelsea bottle' vases, design-number 2, in different sizes and of varying styles of decoration. Any basic shape can occur in many styles. Centre vase $9\frac{3}{4}$ inches high. *c.* 1830–35.

385 A green-ground Minton porcelain vase of shape-number 70, with fine-quality gilding and raised flowers. 19½ inches high. *c.* 1835.

386 A finely modelled and finished Minton 'biscuit'-porcelain portrait-figure of Sir Robert Peel. Figure-design number 77. 11¼ inches high. *c.* 1830–35.

387 A Minton 'biscuit'-porcelain portrait-figure of the Rt. Hon. Charles James Fox. Figure design-number 72. 7¾ inches high. *c.* 1830–35.

318

388 A Minton 'biscuit'-
porcelain 'lacy' figure, one of
several models copied from
Dresden originals. Minton
figure design-number 147. 6
inches high. *c.* 1835–40.

389 A Minton 'biscuit'-
porcelain figure of the
uncrowned Queen Victoria.
Figure design-number 106.
11¼ inches high. *c.* 1837.

opposite page
392 A pair of floral-encrusted Minton porcelain figures in the Dresden style. Minton model-numbers 42 and 43. 7¼ inches high. *c.* 1830.

390 A finely enamelled Minton figure, 'Spanish Guitar Player', design-number 94. 7¼ inches high. *c.* 1830–35.

391 Four typical Minton porcelain figures enamelled in typical styles. Mintons made several animal models, but other firms of the same period produced very similar examples. Central figure—model 84—8¾ inches high. *c.* 1830–35.

393 A superb Minton turquoise-ground plate, jewelled in the Sèvres manner. The portrait of Queen Victoria by Thomas Allen, the flowers by Jesse Smith. This plate was acquired by what is now the Victoria and Albert Museum in 1859.

opposite page
394 A Minton copy of a Sèvres 'Vaisseau à Mat', painted in the style of Morin. Printed mark of the London retailer Mortlock, with date 1881. $17\frac{3}{4}$ inches high.

395 A pair of blue-ground
Minton vases in the fashionable
Sèvres style. One reversed to
show trophy-panel. 15¼ inches
high. *c.* 1862.

396 A Minton vase. Again a
copy of a famous Sèvres shape,
decorated in the finest manner.
Panel by L. Boullemier. 11½
inches high. *c.* 1900.

397 A Minton bottle-vase of a characteristic shape, but decorated with a rare, silvered ground. 14 inches high. Dated 1886.

398 A blue-ground Minton vase of a popular, standard shape. The figure-panel signed by F. N. Sutton. Printed mark in gold. 12½ inches high. *c.* 1900.

Nantgarw

NANTGARW
(*c.* 1817–20)

The story of the Welsh Nantgarw porcelain starts in 1813, when William Billingsley, the well-known Derby-trained ceramic artist, set up with Samuel Walker a small porcelain manufactory at Nantgarw, by the Glamorgan canal, linking with Cardiff and the Bristol Channel. Porcelain production is, however, costly and extremely risky, and soon the available funds of the potters and their backers (chiefly William Weston Young) had been exhausted. After appealing for Government help in 1814, the experiments were continued at the Swansea factory under Lewis Weston Dillwyn (see page 398). In December 1816 Billingsley, later Walker and Young, returned to Nantgarw and successfully re-started their old works.

Most marked Nantgarw porcelain is of the 1817–20 period, after which it is believed (but not proved) that Billingsley and Walker left to be employed by John Rose of the Coalport factory. Certainly Billingsley was buried, under his assumed name Beely, at Kemberton near Coalport on 19 January 1828, in his seventieth year. William Weston Young remained at Nantgarw for a period of two years, probably glazing and decorating, with Thomas Pardoe, some of the remaining Nantgarw porcelains, but it is unlikely that any new wares were made after Billingsley left in 1820. A final sale of china, moulds, etc., was advertised on 28 October 1822.

While the Nantgarw porcelain is soft and translucent, it is normally rather more thickly potted than the related Swansea wares and the decoration is generally rather more simple, although much was sold to London decorators, and such pieces may be ornately decorated. While tea wares were not normally marked, plates, dishes, and other dessert wares often (but by no means invariably) bear the standard impressed mark 'NANT-GARW', usually over the initials CW (for China Works), although the two-word place-name is sometimes written without the hyphen. While the painted name-mark can occur, it is more often found on reproductions. Nantgarw porcelains seldom bear a pattern-number, but when they do occur, they are of simple progressive form, not reaching one thousand.

The standard reference-books are: *The Pottery and Porcelain of Swansea and Nantgarw* by E. Morton Nance (B. T. Batsford, London, 1942) and *Nantgarw Porcelain* by W. D. John (Ceramic Book Co., Newport, Mon., 1948. Supplement 1956).

399 A detail of a Nantgarw porcelain dish shown against the light to show clearly the standard impressed name-mark and the good, translucent body.

400 A rare—perhaps unique—library writing-set bearing the impressed 'Nant-garw C.W.' mark. Tray 14¾ inches wide. *c.* 1817–20.

401 An impress-marked 'Nantgarw C.W.' porcelain dish from the Mackintosh service, the painting and gilding probably added at one of the London decorating establishments. Diameter 9½ inches. *c.* 1817–1820.

402 Representative pieces from a Nantgarw porcelain tea service. The cup-handles are noteworthy, but the other shapes have near parallels in Coalport porcelain. The plate bears the standard impressed mark. *c.* 1817–20.

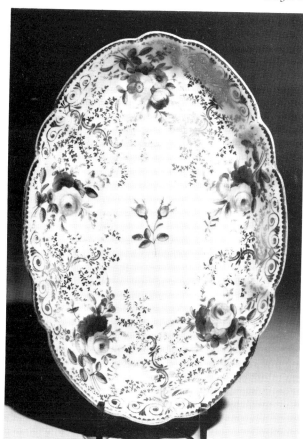

403 An impress-marked Nantgarw dessert dish of typical shape and of a very translucent body. $11\frac{1}{2} \times 8$ inches. *c.* 1817–20.

404 A trio of saucer, tea and coffee cup, the very fine, translucent body decorated in a typical Welsh style. The handle-form is characteristic. The saucer does not have a foot-rim. *c.* 1817–20.

New Hall

NEW HALL
(*c.* 1781–1835)

The name New Hall was that adopted by a group of Staffordshire potters who acquired Richard Champion's patent rights to manufacture a type of hard-paste porcelain using Cornish china clay and china stone, as had been used previously at the Bristol factory. Richard Champion (of Bristol) was in Staffordshire from November 1781 to April 1782, having sold the remaining rights (the patent lapsed in 1796) to an enterprising group of Staffordshire potters of whom the most important were John Turner,[1] Anthony Keeling,[1] Samuel Hollins, John Daniel, and Jacob and Peter Warburton. These potters traded under various names such as 'Hollins, Warburton & Co.' but today the accepted name is New Hall china, this being adopted on account of the factory-site at the New Hall at Shelton in the Staffordshire Potteries.

To most collectors the name New Hall brings to mind rather cottage floral-patterned tea wares. But while this factory did produce such porcelains, so did practically every other manufacturer of the period. Rather than show a selection of these familiar wares, I illustrate a rather different range of pure New Hall porcelain. The earliest tea wares and tea sets formed the bulk of the output from the factory, were attractively decorated with simple gilt designs (Plates 405–6). The so-called silver-shape teapot was not introduced for several years, and the earliest New Hall pots are globular or have a circular plan (Plates 406 and 408). A rather rare early silver-shape teapot has attractive, applied rosette feet (Plate 407). One of the standard silver-shape teapots (without feet) is shown in Plate 410 with related wares, but here also the design is not the familiar, simple floral motif, but rather a blue and gold pattern.

The cream- or milk-jugs illustrated in Plates 409 and 411 show a range of typical New Hall shapes and designs. The covered jug shown in Plate 412 was painted by Fidelle Duvivier, a talented artist employed in the late 1780s. Examples of his painting are scarce; they normally include kilns in the background. The flower-painting on the presentation jug (Plate 413) is peculiar to New Hall, the roses usually showing a kidney-shaped section.

The teapot depicted in Plate 414 is printed in gold and bears the written mark 'Warburton's Patent' under a crown. The Patent was taken out in February 1810 and a most attractive range of New Hall wares was bat-printed in this style during

[1] These two potters soon retired from the New Hall concern, but they continued to make wares under their own names, producing mainly pottery.

330

the 1810–12 period. The gilt, fluted tea wares shown in Plate 415 are typical of the 1800–1810 period and are of the type often erroneously called Chamberlain-Worcester. The tea wares shown in Plate 416 are likewise not readily recognised as New Hall, but they represent rare forms of the 1805–10 period.

That the New Hall hard-paste body was continued to at least 1811 is evidenced by a jug in the author's collection, but soon after this, probably in 1812, the porcelain was changed to the standard white bone-china body. This was often more thinly potted and the glaze was more even. Though most of these later bone-china wares were unmarked except for the pattern-number, some bear the printed mark shown to the right.

Some most attractive bat-printed designs appear at this period, see Plates 417–18. Little is known of the 1820–35 New Hall wares, and it would seem at this later period that the New Hall porcelains lost their individuality.

The New Hall pattern-numbers run in simple progressive sequence from 1 (the early wares were very seldom marked so that it is difficult to find the early pattern-numbers) to about 2300. The pre-1812 hard-paste wares may bear pattern-numbers up to about 1050.

The subject of New Hall and its many contemporaries which produced very similar porcelains is a vast one and the reader is recommended to study *New Hall* by D. Holgate (Faber & Faber, London, 1987). David Holgate also contributed the New Hall chapter to the general work *Staffordshire Porcelain* (Granada, 1983). The reader is also referred to A de Saye Hutton's *A Guide to New Hall Porcelain Patterns* (Barrie & Jenkins, London, 1990).

405 An early New Hall covered cream-jug of graceful form, bearing a simple gilt design. Unmarked. 5 inches high. *c.* 1782–85.

406 An early New Hall teapot and stand of a very rare—untypical—shape, bearing a simple, gilt border design, again a style seldom associated with this factory. Teapot 5¼ inches high. *c.* 1782–85.

407 A New Hall hard-paste teapot, an early version of the so-called silver-shape teapot but with rare, applied floret feet. 4¾ inches high. *c.* 1785.

408 An attractive and rather rare New Hall teapot-form decorated with the popular Chinese-style design—Number 20. Note the knob-form. 6½ inches high. *c.* 1785.

409 A simply decorated New Hall creamer of a characteristic shape. Painted pattern-number 167. 5 inches high. *c.* 1785–90.

410 Representative pieces from a blue-and-gold-decorated New Hall hard-paste tea service, showing the typical teapot-form with its stand. Painted pattern-number 153. Teapot 6¼ inches high. *c.* 1785–90.

411 A selection of New Hall hard-paste cream- or milk-jugs, showing various shapes and styles of decoration. *c.* 1785–1810.

412 A rare New Hall hard-paste covered cream- or milk-pot painted by Duvivier, an artist who normally included smoking kilns in the background. Note the characteristic handle-form. 5¼ inches high. *c.* 1782–87.

413 A New Hall hard-paste jug of characteristic form, painted by an artist who often included a rose with a kidney-shaped petal. 6¼ inches high. *c.* 1790–95.

Colour Plate VIII A fine
Minton Parian vase, the pâte
sur-pâte panel worked by
Laurence Birks and signed with
his initial monogram.
Impressed Minton name-mark,
also gold-printed globe and
year-cypher for 1881. $12\frac{1}{2}$ inches
high.

414 A New Hall hard-paste teapot decorated in blue and gold. The scenic panel is decorated by Warburton's patent printing-process, by which gold or other metallic colours could be applied by means of a stipple-print. Written mark 'Warburton's Patent, No. 888' under a crown. $5\frac{1}{4}$ inches high. *c.* 1810–12.

415 Representative pieces from a gilt New Hall hard-paste tea set, showing typical forms of the 1800 period. Pattern-number 270. Teapot $7\frac{1}{2}$ inches high.

opposite page
416 Representative pieces from
a New Hall hard-paste tea set
of the 1805–10 period.
Although these shapes are
characteristic, they are rare.
Painted pattern-number 1085.
Teapot 6 inches high.

417 Representative pieces from
a New Hall bone-china tea
service of the 1815 period.
The black bat-printed motifs
can occur on the earlier hard-
paste body, and in gold
(Warburton's patent), but
several other factories favoured
similar Adam Buck style
designs. Pattern-number 1109.

418 A fine blue-ground New Hall bone-china punch-bowl, printed with coloured-over Adam Buck-style bat-prints. Painted pattern-number 1277. Diameter 9 inches.

419 A relief-moulded New Hall bone-china dessert dish in the style of the 1815–25 period. Painted pattern-number 1707. $9\frac{7}{8} \times 6\frac{5}{8}$ inches.

Parian China

This matt, creamy-white ceramic body was introduced in the early 1840s and remained popular throughout the whole of the Victorian era. The quality is very variable as, after the success enjoyed by the leading manufacturers of this ware, many small firms sought to produce low-priced imitations. These badly designed, poorly finished, pieces made by very small concerns gave the whole range a bad name, but good early Parian made by the leading firms can be superb and most decorative.

We do not know the exact date of the introduction of the Parian body, originally termed 'Statuary Porcelain', but Messrs Copeland & Garrett of Stoke were producing figures in the new ware in 1844 and the example shown on page 28 was ordered in April 1845. This firm's successors, Messrs Copelands, were to become the largest manufacturers of Parian wares, closely rivalled by Mintons, but by 1850 there was scarcely a porcelain manufacturer who was not following the fashion for these reduced copies of classical and Victorian sculpture.

Although the body was introduced to bring such small-sized sculpture within reach of all, its excellent moulding qualities soon became readily apparent, and useful objects—countless jugs—even fireplaces and floral jewellery were soon made in the unglazed Parian. It was extremely versatile. It could be tinted (most pâte-sur-pâte is coloured Parian—see the next section) or glazed, and much Royal Worcester, Belleek, or even Goss china is really glazed Parian.

The few representative examples illustrated here show some of the finer-quality pieces. Other examples are shown in Plates 14, 201–2, but for fuller details the reader is referred to: *Victorian Porcelain* by G. A. Godden (Herbert Jenkins, London, 1961) and *The Illustrated Guide to Victorian Parian China* by C. and D. Shinn (Barrie & Jenkins, London, 1971).

Engraving of Copeland Parian
figures shown at the 1871
Exhibition.

420 A fine Minton Parian
group of Hebe and the eagle,
model-number 339 in the
factory records. Impressed
name-mark. *c.* 1850–55. 22
inches long.

421 A Parian figure made for the Crystal Palace Art Union by Bates, Brown-Westhead & Moore in the 1858–61 period. 15 inches long.

422 A Copeland Parian group of Paul and Virginia. Impressed name-mark with year-mark 76 for 1876. 12 inches high.

423 An imposing but unmarked Parian portrait-figure of Princess Alice. 13¾ inches high. *c.* 1880.

424 A Copeland Parian and glazed porcelain fruit-comport, one of six in a large dessert service. 11¾ inches high. *c.* 1875.

425 An Old Hall Earthenware Company moulded Parian jug of a design registered in April 1862. Thousands of differently designed jugs—often in sets—were made in Parian during the Victorian era. 9½ inches high.

Pâte-Sur-Pâte

PÂTE-SUR-PÂTE
(1870–the present century)

This Victorian technique—'body-on-body'—has the effect of a ceramic cameo. The white (or, rarely, tinted) layers of semi-translucent Parian china are built up layer by layer over a tinted Parian ground, to give, after repeated tooling, a cameo effect. The work is slow and highly skilled, and such work was only produced in limited quantities by leading firms such as Mintons and the Royal Worcester Company.

The technique was introduced at the Sèvres factory in France, and one of the French exponents, Marc Louis Solon, brought his skill to Mintons in 1870. The fine figure-work produced by Solon for Mintons has always been justly respected and expensive. Each Solon composition is unique and signed. Typical pieces can be seen in Plates 426–30, his tall willowy figures being noteworthy. While at Mintons, Solon trained several artists to work in the pâte-sur-pâte technique, these included A. Birks, L. Birks, H. Hollins, T. Mellor, F. Rhead, T. H. Rice, H. Sanders, and C. Toft. The initial- or monogram-marks of these artists will be found, although all such work is very scarce. Alboine Birks produced the most pieces, on account of his long working life—from 1876 to 1937. He, in turn, trained Richard Bradbury, the last of the pâte-sur-pâte artists who worked for Mintons up to the outbreak of the 1939–45 war. Apart from vases and other objects wholly decorated in pâte-sur-pâte, some twentieth-century Minton plates have inset pâte-sur-pâte panels.

While most of the finest pâte-sur-pâte bears the Minton globe mark—often in gold —other firms made excellent pieces. These include: W. Brownfield & Sons of Cobridge, c. 1880; G. Grainger & Co., Worcester, c. 1880–1900; George Jones (& Sons), Stoke, c. 1876–90; Moore Brothers of Longton, c. 1878–90; Royal Worcester Company, c. 1875–90.

The examples found most often were made at George Jones's Crescent Pottery at Stoke-on-Trent. Here the artist was Frederick Schenk and his examples (Plates 433–34) have often been mistaken for Minton pieces. Some of the George Jones examples are unmarked, but often a faintly impressed GJ monogram can be seen in certain lights, though it is often overlooked. The George Jones designs are apt to be repetitive.

For further information on English pâte-sur-pâte (much was also produced in France and at the leading German factories) the reader is referred to: 'English Pâte-sur-Pâte Porcelain' by G. A. Godden, *The Connoisseur*, June 1954, and *Victorian Porcelain* by G. A. Godden (Herbert Jenkins, London, 1961).

426 Minton pâte-sur-pâte by
M. L. Solon, reproduced from
the *Pottery Gazette* of July 1899.
The centre vase was then
priced at eighty guineas.

427 An attractive Minton pâte-sur-pâte vase, signed and decorated by M. L. Solon, the reliefs and gilt enrichments on a deep blue-green-tinted Parian body. Shape-number 1986. Gold-printed globe mark. 15¾ inches high. *c.* 1895–1900.

428 A fine Minton pâte-sur-pâte vase with rare two-colour ground, signed and decorated by M. L. Solon. 23 inches high. *c.* 1890.

429 A black-ground Minton
stained-Parian plate or wall-
plaque, the pâte-sur-pâte motifs
signed 'L Solon'. Gilt globe
mark. Diameter 9⅜ inches.
c. 1895.

430 A unique Minton
garniture or clock set in
blue and celadon-tinted
Parian, the pâte-sur-pâte
designs by M. L. Solon.
Impressed Minton name-mark
with date-cyphers for April
1871. 14½ and 17½ inches high.
These pieces were exhibited at
the London Exhibition of 1871–
1872.

431 A selection of Minton pâte-sur-pâte, unsigned pieces by Solon's apprentices. Impressed and printed Minton marks. Bottle-vase 13 inches high. *c.* 1875–85.

432 A pair of white-ground Minton pâte-sur-pâte 'Games' vases, designed by John Wadsworth and modelled by Richard Bradbury—Minton's last craftsman in this technique. *c.* 1936. 9 inches high.

433 A typical pâte-sur-pâte plaque from George Jones's Crescent Pottery at Stoke-on-Trent, worked by Frederick Schenk. Impressed mark. *c.* 1888. Diameter 13¼ inches.

434 A pair of olive-green-ground George Jones pâte-sur-pâte vases of a type often sold as Minton. Pattern number 5659 in gold. *c.* 1885. 10½ inches high.

350

Pinxton

PINXTON
(1796–1813)

The Pinxton porcelain factory was quite a modest one (employing not more than fifty persons) situated in Derbyshire, some fifteen miles north-west of Derby, on the borders of Nottinghamshire. In many respects, the early Pinxton porcelains of the 1796–99 period are extremely similar in body—and in the soft mellow glaze—to the Derby wares of the same period. This fact is not surprising, for William Billingsley of Derby gave his all-important practical experience to the local John Coke. Several interesting letters from Billingsley to Coke relate to the setting up of the Pinxton factory, and these are reproduced in *The Pinxton China Factory* (privately published, 1963), a work based on the researches of the late C. L. Exley.

Apart from the Derby-like body and covering glaze, the Pinxton shapes offer a very good guide to origin, and representative forms are here shown in Plates 435–45, with further wares featured in the *Illustrated Encyclopaedia of British Pottery and Porcelain*. The tea and coffee services (and most examples found today come from such sets) included straight-sided coffee-cans, the characteristic feature of which is the indented handles (Plate 435). The Pinxton shapes are far more important for identification than the patterns, for in several cases *very* similar designs were employed at other factories—notably Mintons (compare Plate 436 with the mugs shown in Plate 369, a design agreeing with the Minton factory pattern-books).

In April 1799 William Billingsley, the works manager, left Pinxton to set up his decorating establishment at Mansfield, six miles away. Unfortunately, the surviving account-books stop at this period, and the subsequent activities of John Coke & Co. are not at all clear. It would seem that John Coke remained the sole owner until September 1801 when he took as a partner Henry Bankes, who infused fresh funds. This partnership was dissolved in January 1803, after which John Cutts continued the works until 1813. What is unknown is whether porcelain was made at Pinxton after 1803, or if Cutts, a landscape-painter, used the works solely as a decorating establishment, finishing old blanks and buying other wares from Coalport and Staffordshire to decorate. Certainly, several examples featured as Pinxton in various books have every appearance of being of Coalport manufacture.

Very few pieces bear a factory-mark—rare examples bear the name Pinxton—others the painted initial P in script. The porcelain often bears letters of small size impressed with printer's-type, but such letters also occur on Derby porcelain of the same period. The useful table wares often bear a painted pattern-number, sometimes prefixed N or P, as shown, but these numbers are relatively low (they range upwards to only about 400) and are non-fractional. It is possible that some Pinxton porcelain was sold in the white and was subsequently decorated by others, including Billingsley, who was at Mansfield during the 1799–1803 period.

The reader is referred to: *The Pinxton China Factory* by C. L. Exley (published privately by Mr and Mrs R. Coke-Steel, 1963); *English Porcelain, 1745–1850*, edited by R. J. Charleston, Pinxton chapter by A. L. Thorpe (E. Benn, London, 1965); *William Billingsley, 1758–1828* by W. D. John (Ceramic Book Co., Newport, Mon. 1968); *The Connoisseur* magazine of January and February 1963 also contains interesting illustrated articles on Pinxton porcelain.

435 A gilt Pinxton porcelain coffee-can of the type included in most tea sets. This example illustrates the typical, indented Pinxton handle-form. Painted pattern-number 283. *c.* 1795. $2\frac{3}{8}$ inches high.

436 A typical Pinxton porcelain teapot with simple gilding and an enamelled scenic panel. Unmarked, but pattern 300. $5\frac{3}{4}$ inches high. *c.* 1795–1800.

437 A further typical Pinxton porcelain-teapot shape, bearing a pattern also found on Minton wares (see Plate 369). The lid is turned to show the lack of flange and the unglazed edge. Impressed letter Y. 4¾ inches without cover. *c.* 1795–1800.

438 A rare Pinxton scenic-painted bowl and a matching plate. The bowl with impressed letter Z. Diameter 6¼ inches high. *c.* 1800.

439 Representative pieces from
a Pinxton tea set painted in a
typical style. The shapes of the
main pieces are characteristic,
and the coffee-can handles are
of the form shown in Plate
435. Teapot 6 inches high.
c. 1795.

440 A Pinxton sugar-bowl and cover with a teapot stand, the latter reversed to show the unglazed, flat base and the characteristic mark of the support. Pattern-number 312. Sugar-bowl 5¼ inches high. *c.* 1800.

441 Pinxton porcelains of characteristic shapes, decorated with a popular sprig design. The handle-forms are noteworthy. Teapot 6 inches high. *c.* 1795–1800.

442 A Pinxton creamer of a rather rare form, marked with an incised E. 5 inches high. *c.* 1795.

443 A Pinxton porcelain creamer of a characteristic shape; the handle-form should be noted. Painted pattern-number 312. 4½ inches high. *c.* 1800.

357

444 A selection of unglazed Pinxton 'wasters' from the factory-site, now housed at the Victoria and Albert Museum.

445 A bulb-pot of a characteristic Pinxton shape, the flower-panel probably by William Billingsley. The pale, rather spotty, ground colours are noteworthy and may be likened to a water-colour wash. 5 inches high. *c.* 1795–1800.

Plymouth

PLYMOUTH
(*c.* 1768–70)

Plymouth porcelain is, like that of the related Bristol factory, of the true or hard-paste variety. Its manufacture at this West of England port is due to the work of the Quaker chemist William Cookworthy (b. 1705). Correspondence shows that as early as 1745 Cookworthy was interested in the manufacture of porcelain (then hardly established in England), using American raw materials and emulating the Chinese production methods. However, production on a commercial scale did not apparently commence until 1768, after the necessary deposits of the all-important petunste and kaolin had been found in Cornwall. A patent in Cookworthy's name dates from 17 March 1768, and one small inscribed mug, decorated in underglaze-blue, pre-dates the patent by three days.

The Plymouth works closed in 1770—probably in November—after which the employees and working materials were transferred to Castle Green, Bristol (see page 75). Owing to the very brief working of this factory the Plymouth products are now rare. Useful wares were often decorated in a rather inky-black underglaze-blue, in designs nearly always showing Oriental influence (Plates 446–49). Some-times the underglaze-blue designs were enhanced with overglaze enamels, notably red (Plate 450). Figures and groups of animals and birds were also made and are often found in the white (Plate 451), although originally some of these may have been embellished with non-permanent, unfired colour. Other rare Plymouth figures were enamelled, and a typical set of seasons is shown in Plate 452.

Much Plymouth porcelain is unmarked and is distinguished by the hard body and glaze (often somewhat smokey) or by the blackish tint of the underglaze-blue. The factory-mark, when there is one, is the chemist's sign for tin, the numerals 2 and 4 joined. This device was sometimes hastily written (see Plate 446). Plymouth figures can bear the sign 'T' or 'T^{o}', relating to a much-travelled modeller or 'repairer' (the name given to the workman who builds the completed figure from the separately moulded component parts), often referred to as 'Tebo', but recent research suggests that this sign on Bristol, Bow, Caughley, Plymouth, and Worcester porcelains was used by a member of the Toulouse family. Research continues on this subject, but these 'T' or 'T^{o}' marks do occur on Plymouth figures of the 1768–70 period.

For further details the reader is referred to: *Cookworthy's Plymouth and Bristol Porcelain* by F. Severne Mackenna (F. Lewis, Leigh-on-Sea, 1947) and *English Blue and White Porcelain* by B. Watney (Faber & Faber, London, 1963).

446 A blue and white
Plymouth porcelain patty-pan,
showing a rather badly written
version of the standard mark,
the numbers 2 and 4 joined—
the chemist's sign for tin.
Diameter 3¾ inches. *c.* 1768–72.

447 A Plymouth hard-paste
porcelain tankard painted in
the Chinese style in underglaze
blue. 4⅝ inches high. *c.* 1768–
1772.

Colour Plate IX A page from the Wedgwood catalogue of *c.* 1923, showing typical 'Fairyland lustre' designs on characteristic shapes—with the relevant pattern-numbers.

Z 4968
Peche Melba Centre

Z 4968
2409 Shape, Vase
14″

Z 5125
Octagon Bowl
12″

Z 4968,   2308 Shape, Vase, s/s

448 Three Plymouth hard-paste examples painted in typical styles in underglaze-blue. Tankard 6½ inches high. *c.* 1768–72.

449 A Plymouth hard-paste porcelain creamer painted in a typical blue-black underglaze colour. 3¾ inches high. *c.* 1768–72.

450 A moulded Plymouth sauce-boat of characteristic shape, painted in the typical blue-black colour with overglaze red enamel. $5\frac{1}{2}$ inches long. *c.* 1768–72.

451 A pair of white Plymouth figures, the bases of a typical form—also found in Longton Hall. $5\frac{7}{8}$ and $6\frac{1}{4}$ inches high. *c.* 1770.

452 A rare set of Plymouth hard-paste porcelain Seasons, showing typical bases. $5\frac{1}{2}$ and $5\frac{5}{8}$ inches high. *c.* 1770.

Ridgway

RIDGWAY
(c. 1808–55)

Like other potters, the Ridgways—Job, and later his two sons John and William—first made pottery only. The lengthy story of the Ridgways is a complicated one, but here in our consideration of porcelain we are, in the main, concerned with John Ridgway, who was to become 'Potter to Her Majesty Queen Victoria'.

John's father, Job Ridgway, had been trained at the Swansea and the Leeds potteries, after which, in November 1781, he returned to his native Hanley in the Staffordshire Potteries. John, his eldest son, was born in 1786, and William in the following year. The now-famous Cauldon Place Works at Shelton (Hanley) was built in 1802. In 1808 Job took his two sons into partnership, and in this year the manufacture of porcelain was added to that of the standard earthenwares. These early Ridgway porcelains are generally unmarked, but some rare pieces bear the impressed mark 'Ridgway & Sons'. This mark pre-dates Job Ridgway's death in 1813. The rare single-word mark 'Ridgway' normally indicates a date after 1813.

After their father's death in 1813 John and William continued trading in partnership at the Cauldon Place Works until 1830 when the brothers separated. John retained the Cauldon Place factory where much fine porcelain was produced, while William concentrated mainly on the production of various earthenwares at the Bell Works and at other works. The Ridgway porcelain produced by the two brothers in partnership between 1813 and 1830 is of very fine quality, being a compact, rather heavy bone china of pure colour, covered with a close-fitting, clear glaze which very seldom crazed. The decoration can be extremely rich and is always of excellent quality.

While the standard table wares are unmarked at this period, the shapes tend to be characteristic, and special attention should be paid to them (see Plates 455–60). Fortunately, several of the original Ridgway pattern-books (Plate 461) have been preserved, and these enable us, not only to identify the unmarked wares, but also to understand the system of pattern-numbering employed by the Ridgways. These pattern-numbers are listed at the end of this section.

After the two brothers dissolved their partnership, John continued to make fine-quality bone china at the Cauldon Place Works, and in the late 1830s he began to use a printed Royal Arms mark incorporating the initials JR. These initials are, however, very small, and are often missed by people not expecting to find them placed in the ribbon directly under the Royal Arms. On cups and other small wares a crown appears in place of the large armorial mark.

364

In general, the post-1830 John Ridgway porcelains are very similar to the earlier pieces; the same series of pattern-numbers were continued and the characteristic shapes (see Plates 462–64) are identified by means of the surviving factory pattern-books or by reference to marked examples.

John Ridgway specialised in the production of fine-quality bone-china table wares—mainly tea and dessert services. Very few purely ornamental pieces were made, and by the time of the 1851 Exhibition the Cauldon Place factory must have produced more of these porcelain services than practically any other factory. However, as they are generally unmarked, such Ridgway porcelains are often attributed to other, more fashionable, factories, such as Rockingham.

In 1856 the Cauldon Place Works were continued by a new partnership, that of Ridgway, Bates & Co., to be followed by Bates, Brown-Westhead & Moore (1859–1861), Brown-Westhead, Moore & Co. (1862–1904), Cauldon Ltd (1905–20), and Cauldon Potteries Ltd (1960–62), after which the porcelain side of the Cauldon firm was carried on by Coalport China Ltd. The present firm of Ridgway Potteries Ltd is a somewhat distant relative of the William Ridgway firm which was established after the brothers separated in 1830.

The system of pattern-numbering is individual to the Ridgways. During the 1808–55 period, the dessert and dinner services bore straightforward pattern-numbers ranging from approximately 400 to at least 9014 (this sequence most probably continued to 9999). In the mid- or late 1840s a new series of dessert-service pattern-numbers was started, expressed under the number 6. The fine service shown in Plate 464, for example, bears the pattern-number $\frac{6}{3296}$. However, during the same period, the tea wares were marked with fractional numbers, firstly 2/1 to 2/9999, to be continued in a new series expressed under the number 5. The ornamental wares, including ornate 'cabinet' cups and saucers, bear pattern-numbers expressed under the number 3. The Ridgway pattern-numbers are always boldly painted and can hardly be missed.

Few Ridgway porcelains are illustrated in the standard reference-books, but some key pieces, with further representative pages from the pattern-books, are featured in the *Illustrated Encyclopaedia of British Pottery and Porcelain* (Herbert Jenkins, London, 1966). The reader is also referred to *Staffordshire Porcelain*, edited by Geoffrey Godden (Granada, 1983). A comprehensive range of the Ridgway products is shown in *Ridgway Porcelains* by G. A. Godden (Antique Collectors' Club, 1985).

453 A blue-ground Ridgway porcelain jug with white reliefs. Impressed mark 'Ridgway'. 5¾ inches high. *c.* 1810–15.

454 An early Ridgway porcelain punch-bowl decorated with a popular pattern in underglaze-blue and overglaze green and gold. Pattern-number 487. Diameter 11¾ inches. *c.* 1810–15.

opposite page
455 A fine, blue-ground Ridgway porcelain ice-pail and cover, richly gilt. Painted pattern-number 1079. 13½ inches high. *c.* 1815–20.

457 Representative pieces from a Ridgway porcelain tea set of the 1815–20 period, showing characteristic shapes. The Rockingham and Grainger factories produced similar sets. Pattern-number 2/1069. Teapot 5½ inches high.

opposite page
456 Representative pieces from a Ridgway porcelain dessert service of the 1810–15 period, showing characteristic shapes. Pattern-number 747. Centrepiece 13 inches long.

458 A relief-moulded Ridgway plate; the characteristic moulding is found also on tea and other wares. Pattern-number 893. Diameter 8¾ inches. *c.* 1820.

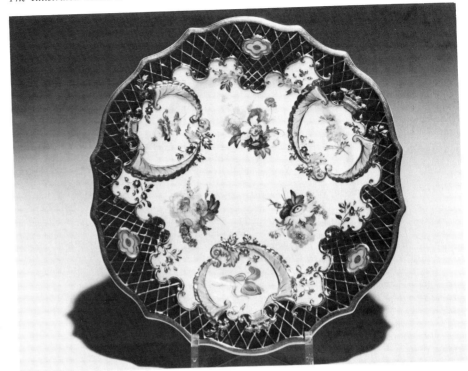

459 Representative pieces from a blue-ground Ridgway dessert service, showing characteristic shapes. Covered tureen. 6 inches high. *c.* 1820–25.

460 Representative pieces from a blue-bordered Ridgway tea service of the 1820s, showing characteristic shapes. Pattern-number 2/1380. Teapot 7 inches high.

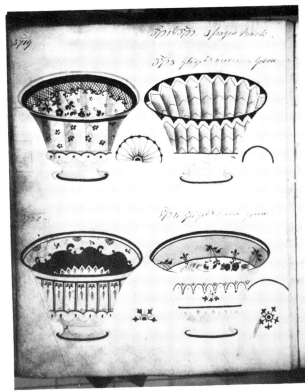

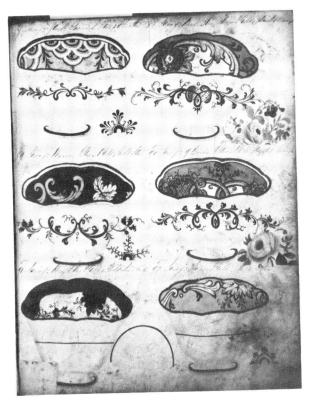

opposite page
461 Four sample pages from the Ridgway pattern-book, showing mainly typical cup-forms.

462 A John Ridgway porcelain tureen, cover, and stand from a large dinner service of the 1845–50 period. Printed Royal Arms mark incorporating the initials J.R. 10 inches high.

463 A John Ridgway porcelain teapot of the 1830s, showing a typical form of the period. Unmarked except for painted pattern-number 2/2208. $10\frac{1}{4}$ inches long.

following page
464 A red-and-gold-bordered John Ridgway porcelain dessert set of the type often erroneously called Rockingham. Unmarked except for the painted fractional pattern-number 6/3296—an impossible pattern-number for the Rockingham factory. Centrepiece $8\frac{3}{4}$ inches high. *c.* 1850.

Rockingham

ROCKINGHAM
(*c.* 1826–42)

Firstly, it must be stated that Rockingham is not a town name, nor is it the name of the manufacturers of these Yorkshire wares. The name relates solely to Earl Fitzwilliam, Marquis of Rockingham, on whose estate the factory was situated. The more correct name for these Rockingham wares would be Brameld, after the potters (John and William) who worked this pottery in the nineteenth century, using the trading-title 'Brameld & Co.' During the period when porcelain was made (1826–42), the works were managed by John Brameld's sons, Thomas, George Frederick, and John Wager Brameld.

The name 'Rockingham' has always been esteemed by collectors of English porcelain, and consequently, much unmarked porcelain has been unjustifiably attributed to these works. The dessert service shown opposite (of Ridgway make) is more in keeping with the general idea of the Rockingham style than some of the marked specimens shown in Plates 465–78, and some wares bearing post-1842 registration-marks (see, for example, Plates 4–8) are very often confused with the earlier Rockingham wares. It must be borne in mind that the period of porcelain manufacture at the Yorkshire factory was a mere sixteen years and that the proprietors were not the only ones to produce rococo-styled tea wares. A host of unmarked Staffordshire figures, animal models, and cottages are popularly and incorrectly ascribed to this quite small factory. In fact, if all the ceramics attributed to the Rockingham factory had been made there, the factory would have overflowed the not inconsiderable county of Yorkshire!

But we should consider what was made by the Bramelds. Much of the porcelain was quite simply decorated on non-rococo forms—witness Plates 465–66. A saucer is reversed in Plate 465 to show the standard 'Griffin' mark and it should be noted that in Rockingham tea services only the saucers were marked. Plates 468–71 show designs more in keeping with the popular idea of Rockingham porcelains, and here the key shapes should be noted—also the marked saucers. A fine range of baskets was made (see Plate 472 and Colour Plate XI of the *Illustrated Encyclopaedia of British Pottery and Porcelain*), also vases. Two standard Rockingham vase-forms are shown in Plates 474–75. The quite rare Rockingham figures are here represented by the single 'biscuit' example, but other recorded examples are featured in the standard books subsequently listed.

The Rockingham bone-china-type porcelain appears somewhat softer than the standard Minton-Ridgway-Spode body, and the glaze has a tendency to form very

fine crazing. Apart from the characteristic shapes—which should be very carefully compared—the best guide is the range of pattern-numbers to be found on the table porcelains. These numbers, which occur without prefix, range from about 410 to about 850 for dessert services, and for tea services, from about 407 to about 1600, followed by a short fractional series running from $\frac{2}{1}$ to about $\frac{2}{150}$. Porcelains with pattern-numbers above two thousand or above $\frac{2}{500}$ cannot be of Rockingham origin, however strong the family tradition which supports the belief. Apart from the printed marks, two typical examples of which are reproduced, some mainly ornamental wares will bear gilt signs of unknown significance, comprising the initials CI, followed by a number. The pre-1831 mark was printed in red or in puce from 1831 to 1842.

It should be noted that the printed Griffin mark can occur on fakes and that the name 'Rockingham' was often employed by other manufacturers, chiefly to denote a dark-brown streaky glaze. It should be borne in mind that this factory made far more earthenwares than porcelains.

Four modern specialist books give very good accounts of the history of the Rockingham Pottery and illustrate a very good range of the products: *The Rockingham Pottery* by A. A. Eaglestone and T. A. Lockett (published by the Rotherham Municipal Libraries and Museum Committee, 1964)[1], *Rockingham Ornamental Porcelain* by D. G. Rice (published by the Adam Publishing Co., London, 1965, and available from the Ceramic Book Co., Newport, Mon.), and *The Illustrated Guide to Rockingham Pottery and Porcelain* by D. G. Rice (Barrie & Jenkins, London, 1971) and *Rockingham Pottery & Porcelain 1745–1842* by Alwyn and Angela Cox (Faber & Faber, London, 1983).

[1] Revised edition published by Messrs David & Charles in 1973.

465 Representative pieces from an attractively simple Rockingham gilt tea set. The shapes are characteristic and the red-printed griffin mark with pattern-number 457 is shown on the reversed saucer. Teapot 5½ inches high. *c.* 1830.

466 A Rockingham porcelain creamer of characteristic shape but decorated in a simple design not normally associated with this factory. Pattern-number 618. 3½ inches high. *c.* 1830.

467 A green-and-gold-bordered Rockingham creamer of a rare but characteristic shape. 3¼ inches high. *c.* 1830.

468 Three Rockingham porcelain jugs, two of which bear the griffin mark printed in puce. Part of the fine collection of Rockingham on view at the Rotherham Museum. Centre jug 8 inches high. *c.* 1835–40.

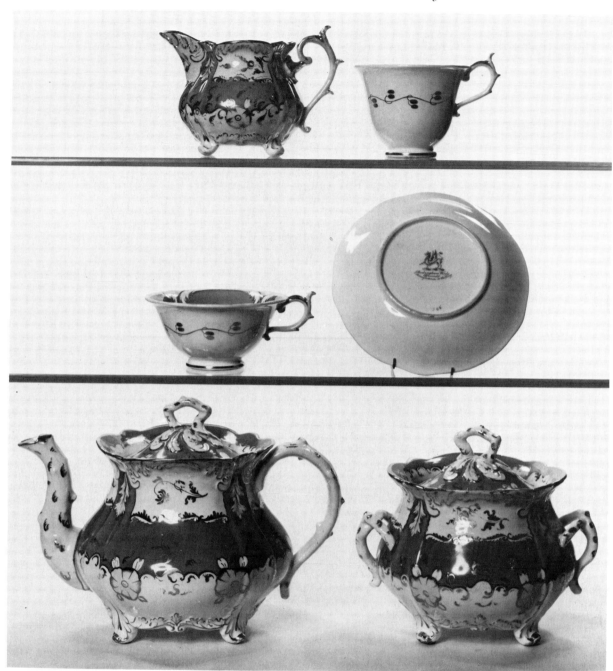

469 Representative pieces from a green and gold Rockingham porcelain tea set, of the type normally associated with this Yorkshire factory. The standard puce-printed griffin mark is seen on the reversed saucer—only the saucers being marked, a standard practice at this factory. Pattern-number 986. Teapot 6¼ inches high. *c.* 1835.

470 A typical Rockingham covered sugar-bowl decorated in grey and gold. Note the crown-shaped knob, a feature found on related Rockingham teapots. Pattern-number 1170. $4\frac{3}{4}$ inches high. *c.* 1840.

471 Representative pieces from a puce and gold Rockingham tea set, the reversed saucer showing the typical puce-printed griffin mark and the late, high pattern-number 1322. The plate is one of a pair of bread-and-butter or cake plates; the sets at this period did not include personal tea plates. Plate $10\frac{1}{2} \times 9\frac{1}{2}$ inches. *c.* 1840–42.

472 A fine griffin-marked
Rockingham porcelain basket
painted with a view of
Brighton. 13 inches long.
c. 1830–35.

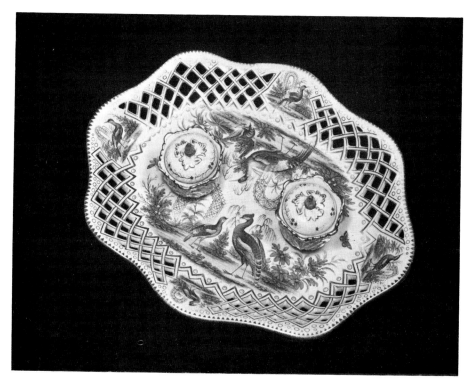

473 A fine and rare griffin-
marked Rockingham inkstand.
15 × 12 inches *c.* 1835.

474 A set of Rockingham porcelain vases of a characteristic form—found decorated in different styles. Griffin mark printed in puce. Centre vase 14⅝ inches high. *c.* 1835.

475 A fine set of floral-encrusted Rockingham porcelain vases, illustrating a further characteristic shape. Griffin mark printed in puce. 14 and 10½ inches high. *c.* 1835.

476 Representative pieces from a rare Rockingham dessert service painted in grey and gold. Griffin mark printed in puce with pattern-number 750. Centrepiece $7\frac{1}{4}$ inches high. *c.* 1835–40.

477 A Rockingham tureen from a dessert service, illustrating a further characteristic shape. $9\frac{1}{2}$ inches long. *c.* 1835.

478 A good-quality and typical Rockingham biscuit (unglazed) porcelain figure. Impressed griffin mark, also 'Rockingham Works Brameld' and incised number 4. 6 inches high. *c.* 1830.

Colour Plate X A fine large porcelain version of the well known figure of Eloquence or St. Paul preaching. The model occurs in Wood's earthenware and this unmarked porcelain example is almost certainly an example of his rare porcelain. 17 inches high *c.* 1800. An earthenware version is in the Schrieber Collection at the Victoria and Albert Museum (see N.310 in vol. II of the catalogue). Impressed marked 'E. Wood' examples are also known.

Spode

SPODE
(c. 1797–1833)

The first Josiah Spode (1733–97) was apprenticed in 1749 to the famous potter, Thomas Whieldon. When Spode established his own pottery at Shelton in about 1761 and from about 1764 at Stoke, he produced only pottery, some very fine basalt wares, and, perhaps, salt-glazed white wares. In the early 1770s he traded in partnership with Thomas Mountford and with William Tomlinson. It is to the second Josiah Spode (1755–1827) that we owe the introduction of the now world-famous English bone china. In about 1778 Josiah Spode II established himself as a dealer in earthenwares, porcelains, and glass in London, but after his father's death in August 1797, he returned to Stoke-on-Trent to manage the pottery.

While we have no firm evidence of the date on which the Spode factory introduced the production of porcelain, it was probably at this period, and it was no doubt prompted by the need to make sophisticated china tea wares capable of withstanding hot liquid. Because the prohibitive duties resulted in the almost total cessation of the importation of Chinese porcelain, various former retailers and potters turned their attention to meeting the requirements of the porcelain-buying public. The early Spode porcelain wares are seldom marked, although most examples bear a pattern-number. The body is pure white and compact, with a good close-fitting glaze, and the quality of the potting is always neat and workmanlike.

The porcelain table wares shown in Plate 479 represent a popular early design, number 282, some pieces of which bear the rare impressed mark 'Spode'. The tea wares shown in Plate 480 represent characteristic shapes of the 1800–1805 period, although somewhat similar forms were produced at Coalport (see Plates 161 and 165). The bases are flat, very often showing the whorls caused by the wire used to separate the object from the spinning wheel-head, and are wiped nearly clear of glaze. The flange of the Spode teapot-lid is unique to this period, as is the inside edge of the teapot—features shown in Plate 480. The Spode cup-handle form is also characteristic and is shown in Plate 482. This handle was employed over some fifteen years, and after noting that it can, very rarely, appear in hard-paste New Hall porcelain, one can regard it as a firm indication of a Spode origin. Many early Spode patterns of the 1797–1820 period were achieved by the bat-printed process (see Plate 481).

By 1810 the standard tea-ware shapes had changed to the 'canoe', a teapot of which is shown in Plate 483 (with other representative pieces of matching shapes being shown in the *Illustrated Encyclopaedia of British Pottery and Porcelain*, Plate 534).

This finely gilt teapot and stand exists with the original account dated 1810. By this period the porcelains were normally given the written name-mark 'Spode' accompanied by the pattern-number, and unmarked Spode porcelains of the period are very rare.

The often richly decorated porcelains of this period, in fact up to 1822, owe their embellishments to a separate decorating establishment within the Spode factory, an establishment owned and managed by Henry Daniel. In this apparently unique arrangement, the Spode factory was responsible only for making the porcelain—the Daniels for the decoration. In August 1822 this arrangement was terminated and the Daniels, with some of the decorators, established their own factory at Stoke (see page 186).

Among the most popular of the Spode-styles were the gay 'Japan' patterns, with underglaze-blue used in conjunction with overglaze red and green enamels and gilding. Of several such designs, number 967 is the most popular (see Plates 484–85). Other designs, such as the pheasant (Plate 489), are based on an outline-print coloured in by hand. The quality of the flower-painting can be seen in Plates 490 and 492, while the gilding on the dessert centrepiece (Plate 491) is typically superb.

A new porcelain body containing felspar was introduced in 1821 (John Rose of Coalport had used felspar slightly earlier in his leadless glaze) and a series of printed marks were employed on these fine post-1820 wares, marks which like the two shown include the word 'Felspar'.

On the death of Josiah Spode II in 1827 the factory at Stoke passed to a son of the same name. But Josiah Spode III died two years later in October 1829 and the Spode factory was in the hands of Trustees. In March 1833 both the Spode factory with the stock and working materials and the London retail establishment were purchased by W. T. Copeland for more than fifty thousand pounds. With his new partner, Thomas Garrett, Copeland produced Spode-type wares in the 1833–47 partnership of Messrs Copeland & Garrett, though subsequently he worked under his own name (see page 177).

In this brief summary we have been concerned only with porcelain, but the Spode factory produced a very wide range of earthenwares, including some of the finest of the Staffordshire blue-printed wares and a good selection of the durable stone china. But it should be noted that very few, if any, figures were produced by the Spodes. A very fine representative selection of Spode wares, both pottery and porcelain, is featured in the Spode collectors' bible, *Spode* by Leonard Whiter (Barrie & Jenkins, London, 1989). The book illustrates a useful set of shapes—many from the factory shape-books. Spode pattern-numbers run in simple sequence from the earliest, in about 1797, to pattern 5300 at about the time of the Copeland & Garrett take-over in March 1833. However, some few underglaze designs bear a short series of numbers with the prefix B. These run up to about B450 in the 1833 period, continued in the Copeland & Garrett period to B945.

opposite page
479 Representative pieces from an early Spode porcelain dinner service, showing typical shapes and a popular pattern—number 282. *c.* 1790 (wares at this period seldom bear a name-mark). Oval tureen 5 inches high.

480 Representative Spode porcelain tea wares of the 1790–1800 period, showing characteristic shapes. The inside flange of the teapot and lid, as shown, is noteworthy. Teapots 6¾ inches high. *c.* 1800.

481 A graceful, early Spode porcelain tureen bearing the popular bat-printed pattern-number 500. 6 inches high. *c.* 1805.

482 A colourful Spode 'Japan' pattern—number 715—on a creamer of typical form and a cup and saucer; the cup-handle is a characteristic one. Creamer 5½ inches long. *c.* 1805.

483 A finely gilt Spode teapot
and stand of pattern 1002,
of a standard shape of the 1810
period. For matching shapes see
*An Illustrated Encyclopaedia of
British Pottery and Porcelain*,
Plate 534. The original account
for this service is dated 1810.
Teapot 6$\frac{3}{8}$ inches high.

484 A rare Spode 'Japan'-pattern two-handled covered cup and stand, richly gilt. Painted pattern-number 976. 4½ inches high. *c.* 1810.

485 Representative pieces of a Spode porcelain tea service of the 1810–15 period, showing characteristic shapes. Painted name-mark with pattern-number 1645. Teapot 6¼ inches high.

486 A finely decorated and graceful Spode porcelain bowl (for pot-pourri) with separate pierced cover. Painted name-mark with pattern-number 3234. 7½ inches high. *c.* 1815–1820.

487 A good set of three Spode cachepots, on separate stands. Although these are marked 'Spode' with the pattern-number 382, other factories of the period made such items of similar form. 6½ and 5½ inches high. *c.* 1805.

488 An attractive blue-ground Spode porcelain jug with Wedgwood-styled reliefs. Impressed 'Spode' mark. 5⅜ inches high. *c.* 1805–10.

489 A rare Spode porcelain honey-pot of the popular pheasant pattern (number 2083), being a printed copy of a Chinese design. Spode name-mark with pattern-number. 4½ inches high. *c.* 1810–15.

490 Representatives pieces
from a superb Spode dessert
service, illustrating rare
forms with relief-moulded
borders—richly gilt. The fine-
quality flower-painting is
typical. Tureens 6 inches high.
c. 1815–20.

opposite page
491 A finely gilt Spode
centrepiece from a dessert
service of the 1815 period.
This shape is a characteristic
one. Painted 'Spode' name-
mark with pattern-number
3765. Length 13½ inches.

492 Representative pieces from
a buff and gold Spode dessert
service, showing characteristic
forms of the 1820 period.
Printed 'Spode Felspar' mark
with pattern-number 4373.
Centrepiece 12½ inches long.

493 A Spode dessert dish of typical form. Painted mark Spode, 4033'. $11\frac{1}{4} \times 8\frac{1}{4}$ inches. *c.* 1820.

494 A typically good quality, well decorated Spode porcelain cabinet cup and saucer. The cup with gilt interior. Similar examples were made at the Daniel factory. Painted 'Spode' mark. Diameter of saucer $5\frac{1}{4}$ inches. *c.* 1825–30.

495 Representative pieces from
a fine Spode porcelain dessert
service, showing characteristic
shapes of the 1815–25 period—
shapes to be found decorated
with a multitude of finely
enamelled designs. Centrepiece
12 inches long.

Swansea

Swansea was an important centre of the British ceramic industry, producing in Wales during the eighteenth and nineteenth centuries a good range of earthenwares, of a functional, as well as an ornamental, nature. In this book we are, however, concerned only with the Swansea porcelain, which with the other Welsh porcelains of Nantgarw (page 326) marks the high-water mark of British porcelain for the purity and translucency of the body. The plate shown in Plate 196 has been photographed against a light to illustrate this characteristic, but even without such lighting this porcelain will normally appear very translucent.

In 1814 Lewis Weston Dillwyn of the Swansea 'Cambrian Pottery' invited William Billingsley and Samuel Walker of the Nantgarw Works to join him at Swansea in order to perfect and produce commercially the fine porcelain made at excessive risk and expense at Nantgarw. Success was achieved at Swansea and superb wares were produced between 1814 and 1817, when Billingsley and Walker returned to Nantgarw. Dillwyn's successors, Bevington & Co., continued to decorate old stock and perhaps produce some new porcelain into the 1820s.

The Welsh porcelains, with their highly translucent body and the soft and friendly glaze, proved extremely popular with the London decorators (a most important and little-researched aspect of British ceramics) who purchased the Welsh porcelains in the undecorated state, themselves enamelling the wares in the fashionable styles. Much was, of course, decorated at Swansea and sold in the normal manner, and many very talented artists were employed, including perhaps the finest team of flower-painters ever to work together at any one porcelain factory. These include the talented and much-travelled William Billingsley.

It is impossible here to give more than the briefest outline of the story of Swansea porcelain, and the collector must consult specialist works for a fuller review of the various products, the different bodies, and the talented artists who decorated them. These works include *The Pottery and Porcelain of Swansea and Nantgarw* by E. Morton Nance (B. T. Batsford, London, 1942) and *Swansea Porcelain* by W. D. John (Ceramic Book Co., Newport, Mon., 1958).

An interesting article by A. N. Morgan appears in the American magazine *Antiques* of October 1971. The marks employed comprise the impressed word 'Swansea', often with crossed tridents below. The name 'Dillwyn & Co' can also occur, but it is rare. Overglaze marks include the transferred, red-printed name 'Swansea', which may also be painted by hand. Swansea porcelain has been reproduced over many years, both on the Continent and by English manufacturers, and the overglaze marks should be treated with caution. A study of the character of the porcelain, the shapes, and the decoration is more reliable than the easily faked name-marks. The examples here illustrated are typical, but feature only a small percentage of the known shapes and styles.

The pattern-numbers, found only on the useful table wares, are of simple progressive form, without prefix and will not exceed one thousand.

496 A Swansea porcelain plate photographed against the light to show the fine tranlucency of the Swansea body. The relief-moulded border design, although often used at the Welsh factories, can also occur on Coalport, Davenport, and Derby wares. Diameter 8½ inches. *c.* 1814–22.

opposite page
497 Two Swansea cups and saucers and a plate of a rare and attractive gilt and enamelled design. The cup-handle form is noteworthy. Printed 'Swansea' mark. Diameter of plate 8¼ inches. *c.* 1814–22.

498   A Swansea porcelain tureen and stand, from a dinner service. Impressed mark 'Swansea', with crossed tridents below. Diameter of stand 7½ inches. *c.* 1814–22.

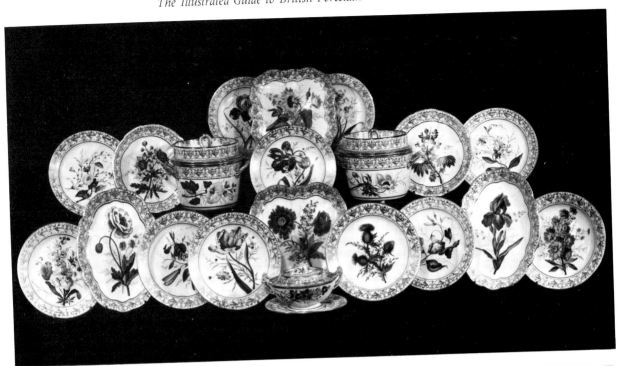

opposite page
499 Representative pieces from the Gosford Castle Swansea porcelain service. The tureen shape is as Plate 498. Most dishes have the impressed Swansea name-mark. Ice-pails 9 inches high. *c.* 1815–20.

500 Representative pieces from a finely and typically painted Swansea dessert service, showing characteristic shapes. Impressed Swansea name-mark on two pieces. Centre dish 14 inches long. *c.* 1815–20.

501 A Swansea cup and saucer decorated in a modest manner but very well potted and with typical handle. Unmarked. *c.* 1815–20.

502 Representative pieces from an attractive relief-moulded Swansea tea service decorated in a simple manner, illustrating characteristic shapes. Painted or stencilled Swansea name-marks. Teapot 5¼ inches high. *c.* 1815–22.

503 Representative pieces from a Swansea tea service, the flower-painting probably by William Pollard. While these shapes, particularly the cup-handles, are characteristic, rather similar forms were used elsewhere, notably at Coalport. Red-stencilled Swansea name-mark. Teapot 6 inches high. *c.* 1815–22.

504 Three Swansea porcelain vases of a characteristic shape, decorated in varying styles. The centre and right-hand vases bear the impressed Swansea name-mark with two crossed tridents under. 10½ inches high. *c.* 1815–22.

Wedgwood

WEDGWOOD
(*c.* 1812–*c.* 1822)

The name Wedgwood is rightly associated with earthenwares, the fine black basalt, the coloured jaspers, and the plainer cream or pearl wares (all of which are featured in the companion volume). However, there were two distinct periods when this firm produced fine-quality bone china.

It is believed that the Wedgwood Company did not produce porcelain before about 1812, when nearly every other important pottery had already turned to this refined body for their more pretentious and expensive lines. That Wedgwoods had hitherto neglected this branch of the trade is probably due to the excellence of their various earthenwares, in the production of which they stood supreme. Nevertheless, for the best tea wares, the refined white translucent porcelain could not be bettered, and in this one field the Wedgwood Company and its retail establishment in London would have been at a disadvantage compared with the rival porcelain manufacturers.

The idea of turning to porcelain may well have been suggested by the reports from the London showrooms, perhaps even by the visit of a rival manufacturer— Miles Mason. The London manager in 1810 reported back to the factory in Staffordshire:

Mr. Mason of Lane Delph [see page 295] is in town and he called upon me and in the course of conversation said that we should sell immence quantities of china— if we had it—and he would be very happy to make it for you. His china is I believe very good and he has great orders for it. . . .

Within about two years the Wedgwood pottery had begun to make porcelain on a relatively small scale, restricting production mainly to tea wares. These are, as one would expect, neatly potted, and have a smooth, creamy feel. The glaze appears to have been whitened with oxide of tin and is close-fitting and thin. The hand-painted landscape-designs are attributed to the former Pinxton artist John Cutts, but many patterns are coloured-in printed designs (Plates 507–8). The mark on the bone china comprises the printed word 'Wedgwood', which can occur in various colours including gold, but is usually in red. Many authorities state that the production of bone china ceased in 1822, but this date is by no means certain. Nevertheless, it was obviously not a commercial success—the rival porcelain manu-

WEDGWOOD

WEDGWOOD

WEDGWOOD
BONE CHINA
MADE IN ENGLAND

facturers perhaps being too well entrenched in this market—and the Wedgwood porcelains are now extremely rare.

In 1878 the production of translucent porcelain began again. It was successful, and has continued until the present time. Apart from standard and tasteful table-ware designs, some fine ornamental porcelains were painted by the former Minton artist Thomas Allen (see Plate 513) and the Minton-style acid-gilding was employed for borders.

Of the various twentieth-century Wedgwood porcelains, the 'Fairy' lustre is note-worthy and has recently received attention from collectors. These 'Fairy' wares, with their 'little people', were introduced in November 1915 and were designed by Miss S. M. Makeig-Jones (1881–1945). Typical examples are here shown in Colour Plate IX and in Plates 511–12. At the same period other more orthodox lustre or iridescent designs were produced on simple, often Chinese-style, classical shapes (Plate 514). Of these designs, the dragon proved very popular, but these wares of the 1915–25 period are based on prints and are not individual.

The post-1878 porcelains normally have a printed mark incorporating the Port-land Vase device. Some of the basic amendments are given; the word 'England' should occur after 1891; the stars appear below the vase from about 1900, the words 'Bone China' not being incorporated in the mark before 1937. It should be noted that the impressed year-letter system was not normally used on Wedgwood porcelain.

There are very many specialist books on the very varied Wedgwood products, the more recent works include *The Dictionary of Wedgwood* by R. Reilly and G. Savage (Antique Collectors' Club, 1980) and *Wedgwood Ceramics 1846–1959* by M. Batkin (R. Dennis, London, 1982), plus Robin Reilly's two volume work *Wedgwood* (Macmillan London Ltd, 1989).

505 A selection of Wedgwood bone-china tea wares; the teapot knob-form is characteristic. Printed Wedgwood name-marks. *c.* 1815.

506 Representative pieces from a Wedgwood bone-china dessert service, illustrating characteristic shapes. Printed name-mark. *c.* 1815.

507 Representative pieces from a Wedgwood bone-china tea service bearing a popular coloured-over printed design. These shapes are characteristic and the knob-form shown in Plate 505 occurs here on a new shape. Wedgwood printed name-mark with pattern-number 566. *c.* 1815.

opposite page
508 A tasteful Wedgwood bone-china cup and saucer, the design being a printed outline coloured in by hand. Printed name-mark. *c.* 1815.

509 A selection of Wedgwood bone-china wares bearing the printed name-mark. Tureen 4¾ inches high. *c.* 1815.

Colour Plate XI An attractive and rare Worcester armorial mug of a typical shape— known as the 'bell-shape' as opposed to the generally later straight-sided, cylindrical examples. Inscribed or armorial pieces are rare—often unique— representing individual orders rather than standard designs. Unmarked. $4\frac{3}{4}$ inches high. c. 1765.

opposite page

510 Representative pieces from a simply gilt Wedgwood bone-china tea service of rather rare form. The standard printed name-mark is seen on the upturned coffee-can. Teapot 6¼ inches high. *c.* 1815–18.

511 A circular dish, or wall-plaque, in Wedgwood porcelain decorated in the 'Fairyland lustre' style. Printed 'Portland' vase mark. Diameter 13¼ inches. *c.* 1920.

512 A good Wedgwood porcelain bowl decorated in the 'Fairyland lustre' style. Printed 'Portland' vase mark, pattern Z 4948. Diameter 10⅜ inches. *c.* 1920.

513 One of a pair of fine-
quality Wedgwood porcelain
vases painted by the former
Minton artist Thomas Allen.
Printed 'Wedgwood. Etruria.
England' mark. 15 inches high.
Dated 1894.

514 A page from the original
Wedgwood catalogue of *c.* 1923,
showing further shapes used for
the lustre wares—including the
dragon designs.

Enoch Wood

ENOCH WOOD
(Early 19th century)

As with Wedgwood, the famous name Wood is associated with earthenwares rather than porcelain. Nevertheless, fine-quality porcelains were apparently made by Enoch Wood (1759–1840) for at least a brief period in the early 1800s.

I use the word 'apparently' since we are not as yet absolutely sure that the porcelains attributed to Enoch Wood were in fact made by him. The mark is strangely ambiguous, comprising the letter W, followed by three asterisks within brackets (see Plate 515). The number of letters could well indicate the 'ood' of 'Wood', and certainly the same mark appears on a good range of earthenwares and basalt ware, indicating that the user of the mark produced a wide selection of ceramics—as did Enoch Wood at the famous Fountain Place Works at Burslem in the Staffordshire Potteries. Yet while these porcelains appear to be of the 1800–1810 period, Enoch Wood had, from 1790 to 1818, traded in partnership as 'Wood and Caldwell', and the W (***) mark does not therefore fit as exactly as one would wish.

I have been unable to attribute this problematical mark to any other pottery and porcelain manufacturer of the period, and though I repeat that there is, as yet, no positive proof that these wares were made by Enoch Wood, I am illustrating a selection of these porcelains in the hope that evidence will be forthcoming to prove the true attribution of this class.

It can be noted that these porcelains were, on occasions, sold in the white to independent decorators and that several pieces of this class appear to have been decorated by William Billingsley, probably at Mansfield, between 1799 and 1803. The covered sugar-bowl from a tea service, illustrated here in Plate 515, was probably decorated at Billingsley's Mansfield studio. The signed 'Billingsley, Mansfield, Nottingham' bulb-pot in the Derby Museum is extremely similar in form to the one marked W (***), shown here as Plate 517.

Pattern-numbers do not appear to have been generally used on these porcelains, but if found, one would expect these numbers to be of simple progressive form and well below 1000. For further information and illustrations of related wares, the reader is referred to *Staffordshire Porcelain*, edited by Geoffrey Godden (Granada, 1983), Appendix VI.

515 A covered sugar-bowl and
stand of Enoch Wood's
porcelain, the stand reversed to
show the 'W (***)' mark found
on this class of porcelain.
Diameter of stand 7 inches.
c. 1805.

516 A rare three-piece flower-
vase or pot-pourri, richly gilt
and with silver-lustre and
bearing the impressed 'W (***)'
mark. 7 inches high.

517 A bulb-pot in porcelain
bearing the impressed 'W (***)'
mark attributed to Enoch
Wood. Although many firms of
the 1790–1810 period made
similar D-shaped pots, this
shape is characteristic of this
class. 6 inches high.

Worcester

WORCESTER
(1751–present day)

The city of Worcester has always been one of the main centres of the porcelain industry. Early in the nineteenth century three major porcelain factories at Worcester—the Chamberlain and the Grainger Companies (see pages 100 and 249) and the Flight factory—continued the noble traditions of the first, the Dr Wall, Worcester Porcelain Company. The superb eighteenth-century Worcester porcelains were made from a very workable body containing soapstone, which could be delicately moulded and thinly turned to produce the trimmest of our eighteenth-century porcelains.

In this work, which is mainly concerned with illustrating characteristic specimens, only a very brief résumé of the background details can be given, but several good and reliable modern books are readily available on the subject. These books are listed on page 418.

The history of Worcester porcelain really dates from the original partnership deeds of 4 June 1751. The main partners or 'inventors' were (Dr) John Wall and William Davis. In 1752 the Bristol porcelain works were acquired and, to quote an advertisement of 24 July 1752, these were 'now united with the Worcester Porcelain Company where, for the future the whole business will be carried on'. The early Bristol and Worcester porcelains are *extremely* similar both in their soapstone body and in their moulded and painted decoration. Recent excavations by Mr Henry Sandon and his team have suggested that many wares formerly believed to be pre-1752 Bristol porcelain can equally well be of Worcester origin.

Much of the early Worcester porcelain was decorated in underglaze-blue, with designs showing the current fashion for Oriental designs. Typical examples are shown in Plates 519–22. The superb relief-moulded shapes are suggested by Plates 521–22 and of the overglaze-decorated examples, Plates 523–25 illustrate the trimly moulded forms of some of the most pleasingly designed table ware ever made. The moulded coffee pot shown in Plate 525 is an example of another Worcester forte, transfer-printing—a technique basically employed to speed production and lower cost by mass-production of the decorative process. But study the quality of the engraving, the attractiveness of the design, and the noble shape of the moulded pot. Both shape and decoration are repetitive and mass-produced, yet not at the expense of taste or quality.

It should be noted that with these wares of the 1750s the so-called tell-tale glaze-free line inside the foot-rim does *not* occur. While it very often appears on Worcester porcelains of the 1760–90 period, it can also occur on Caughley and on some Liverpool porcelains. The wiping clear of glaze inside the foot (it is not caused by glaze shrinkage) was a fairly common practical expedient, and it is by no means a sure indication of a Worcester origin.

Apart from the very popular designs decorated in underglaze-blue (examples that were originally much cheaper than the enamelled patterns), the most famous and typical of the Worcester styles in the 1760–80 period were the scale-blue grounds, the reserve panels being painted with a variety of floral, bird, or rarely, figure subjects. Two 'wasters' from the factory-site, together with a completed cup (Plate 518), illustrate this popular technique and the 'square mark' which is often found on such designs. The whorl and fan patterns (Plates 532–33) are other popular designs incorporating both underglaze-blue and overglaze enamel colours.

The blue-printed designs shown in Plates 534, 536, and Colour Plate XII are patterns which very often bear a series of so-called 'disguised numeral' marks (Plate 535) and these have formerly been incorrectly attributed to the Caughley factory. For the full story of this research the reader is referred to the author's *Caughley and Worcester Porcelain, 1775–1800* (Herbert Jenkins, London, 1969).

In 1783, the original factory was purchased by Thomas Flight. Examples of the Flight period are shown in Plates 537–39, the simply decorated, fluted tea wares being very typical of the changing taste. In 1793 Martin Barr joined Flight, giving rise to the Flight & Barr period (1793–1807). Subsequent changes in partnership and in the name or initial marks employed were Barr, Flight & Barr (B.F.B.) 1807–13, Flight, Barr & Barr (F.B.B.) 1813–40. The quality of these early nineteenth-century Worcester porcelains can be superb, richly painted, and gilt on a compact, clean, well-potted body, with a perfect, craze-free glaze.

In 1840 the Flight, Barr & Barr Company joined with the rival Chamberlain firm, and the two traded from 1840 to 1852 as Chamberlain & Co. (see page 100). In 1852 the Kerr & Binns partnership came into being, and from this, in 1862, R. W. Binns formed the Worcester Royal Porcelain Co. Ltd, a company which still flourishes today and whose quality products are known throughout the world as 'Royal Worcester'.

It should be noted that up until 1840 the Worcester porcelains which were made at the main, or original, factory do *not* bear a pattern-number, although painters' numbers can occur during the 1790–1820 period. The Chamberlain and Grainger functional porcelains made in the same city will normally bear a pattern-number. In the Kerr & Binns period (1852–62) pattern-numbers for table wares ranged from about 5000 to 7247. The post-1862 'Royal Worcester' numbers were:

7248 to 9699   (July 1862 to August 1876)

$\dfrac{B}{1}$ to $\dfrac{B}{1081}$ (August 1876 to May 1883)

$\dfrac{W}{1}$ to $\dfrac{W}{9999}$ (May 1883 to 1913)

$\dfrac{C}{1}$ to $\dfrac{C}{3390}$ (1913 to 1928)

$\dfrac{Z}{1}$ onwards   (from 1928 to present day)

Fortunately, two excellent modern books are available to give the reader a detailed account of both the early and the later Worcester porcelains. Both are by Henry Sandon, the former Curator of the Dyson Perrins Museum at the Worcester factory. The books are *The Illustrated Guide to Worcester Porcelain, 1751–*

1793 (Barrie & Jenkins, London, 1969) and *Royal Worcester Porcelain* (Barrie & Jenkins, London, 1973).

Apart from these two books a visit to the Dyson Perrins Museum at Worcester may be considered a must for all serious collectors. Other helpful specialist books on different aspects of the products include: *Coloured Worcester Porcelain of the First Period* by H. Rissik Marshall (Ceramic Book Co., Newport, Mon., 1954), *English Blue and White Porcelain of the 18th Century* by B. Watney (Faber & Faber, London, 1963), *Worcester Blue & White Porcelain 1751–1790* by L. Branyon, N. French & J. Sandon (Barrie & Jenkins, London, 1989 revised edition), *The Life and Work of Robert Hancock* (dealing extensively with the printed wares by Cyril Cook (Chapman & Hall, London, 1955), and for the later figures *The Sandon Guide to Royal Worcester Figures 1900–1970* (Alderman Press, London, 1987).

518 A Worcester scale-blue-ground cup, with an unglazed 'waster' showing clearly this typical motif. A typical Worcester 'square-mark' is seen on the right, again a 'waster' from the site of the eighteenth-century factory.

519 An early Worcester blue and white tankard with typical spreading foot and Chinese-style design. 4⅞ inches high. *c.* 1750–55.

520 A Worcester teapot and stand, or saucer, of a popular early design—the 'root' pattern, shown with a matching 'waster.' Teapot 3½ inches high. *c.* 1755.

521 An amusing and typical relief-moulded Worcester creamer painted in underglaze-blue. Painter's personal tally-mark under the handle. 2¼ inches high. *c.* 1755.

522 A fine and typically Worcester relief-moulded plate from a tea service, painted in underglaze-blue. Painter's personal tally-mark in blue. Diameter 8 inches. *c.* 1755.

523 A Worcester relief-moulded waste-bowl from a tea service, enamelled with a popular Oriental-style design. Diameter 6½ inches. *c.* 1755.

524 A fine and early Worcester relief-moulded oval bowl or butter-dish, enamelled on each side with a Chinese-style design. 2¾ inches high. *c.* 1750–1755.

421

525 An imposing 'feather-moulded' Worcester coffee pot, decorated with one of many black overglaze printed designs favoured at Worcester. The feather-moulded design is to be found on a good range of Worcester tea wares of the 1755–65 period. 9 inches high. *c.* 1755.

opposite page
526 An attractive and typical Worcester sauce-boat painted in underglaze-blue in the popular Oriental style. Painter's personal tally-mark below handle. 8½ inches long. *c.* 1755–60.

527 An attractively designed relief-moulded Worcester sauce-boat—one of many different moulded designs. Open crescent mark in underglaze-blue. 7 inches long. *c.* 1760.

528 A relief-moulded leaf-shaped dish of a popular form, bearing a clear impression of an underglaze-blue print—one of many attractive floral designs. 10½ inches long. *c.* 1765–70.

529 A Worcester three-compartment shell centrepiece, of which several variations were made. The basic theme is by no means restricted to the Worcester factory. 5 inches high. *c.* 1760–65.

530 A simple but attractive blue-bordered Worcester plate from a dessert service. Open crescent mark in underglaze-blue. Diameter 8¾ inches. *c.* 1765–70.

531 A fine and typical pair of Worcester openwork baskets, the exterior with a rare, pale yellow ground, the interior enamelled with flowers. 10 × 8¾ inches. *c.* 1765–70.

425

532 An attractive water-bottle, originally sold with a basin, of the popular Oriental-inspired 'whorl' pattern in underglaze-blue and enamels. 11 inches high. *c.* 1765.

533 A Worcester teapot illustrating the popular Oriental-inspired 'fan' pattern in underglaze-blue, overglaze red, green, and gold. A matching saucer is here reversed to show the standard Chinese-style mark associated with this pattern. Diameter of saucer 4¾ inches. *c.* 1765–70.

534 A fine blue-printed Worcester punch-bowl of the popular Fisherman pattern more often found on Caughley or Liverpool wares. The characteristic Worcester long, slender fish is marked 'A', the loose, wavy fishing-line 'B' (compare with Plate 77). The 'waster' 'C' is from the Worcester factory-site. Diameter $11\frac{1}{5}$ inches. *c.* 1775–80.

535 'Wasters' from the Worcester factory-site, being tea bowl bases showing the blue-printed, disguised numeral-marks, for long thought to be of Caughley origin.

536 A selection of blue-printed Worcester porcelains of the type formerly attributed to the Caughley factory, designs often found with the disguised numeral-marks. Coffee pot 8¼ inches high. *c.* 1775–1800.

537 A Flight-period Worcester teapot of the popular 'whorl' pattern (see Plate 532). Unmarked. 6½ inches high. *c.* 1783–92.

538 A Worcester oval platter from the celebrated 'Hope' service made for the Duke of Clarence in 1792, the figure-panels painted by John Pennington. Blue-painted 'Flight' crowned mark with a crescent under. 16 inches long.

opposite page

539 Representative pieces from a Flight-period spiral-fluted tea set, decorated in a typical manner with underglaze-blue border. These shapes are characteristic, although rather similar forms were used at the Chamberlain factory and at Coalport. Note especially the teapot knob and handle. Blue-painted 'Flight' mark and a small crescent on some pieces. Teapot 6½ inches high. *c.* 1783–88.

540 A pink-bordered Flight, Barr & Barr-period Worcester tureen from a dinner service, bearing the crest and motto of the Peel family. The shape is characteristic of Worcester. 10½ inches high. *c.* 1813–20.

541 Three richly gilt, salmon-ground Barr, Flight & Barr-period Worcester chimney ornaments. The panels are of unusual subjects—perhaps painted to a special order. Written and impressed marks. 8¼ and 5 inches high. *c.* 1807–1813.

542 Part of a Flight, Barr & Barr Worcester porcelain dessert service of pale lavender ground. The centres variously painted with landscapes, shells, birds, or flowers. The tureen-shape is a characteristic one. Printed and impressed initial-marks. Tureens 9 inches high. *c.* 1813–20.

543 Representative pieces from a Flight, Barr & Barr dessert service decorated with a very colourful 'Japan' pattern. The shapes are characteristic Worcester ones of the period. Printed and impressed initial-marks. *c.* 1813–20.

Colour Plate XII An important Worcester porcelain jug of a typical moulded shape decorated with pale overglaze yellow and panels finely painted with mock Oriental scenes. 10½ inches high. *c.* 1755-60.

544 A pair of Barr, Flight & Barr Worcester *jardinières*, the panels painted with the rare and desirable feather motifs. The grey-marbled ground is a typical style of the period. Written name-and-address marks. 6¼ inches high. *c.*1807–1813.

545 Part of a superb and rare Barr, Flight & Barr-period Worcester desk set, finely painted with shell panels on a grey-marbled ground. Written name-and-address marks. Taper-stick (centre) 2½ inches high. *c.* 1807–13.

546 One of a pair of maroon-ground Flight, Barr & Barr pot-pourri vases, finely painted with scenic panels. Written name-and-address marks. 14 inches high. *c.* 1813–20.

547 A trio of teacup, coffee cup and saucer from a Flight, Barr & Barr Worcester green and gold tea set, showing the fine gilding on even ordinary Worcester sets of the period. The handle-shape is characteristic. *c.* 1813–20.

548 A fine and typical Flight, Barr & Barr claret-ground vase, painted with a 'South West view of Worcester'. Written name-and-address mark. 9¾ inches high. *c.* 1813–20.

opposite page
549 A pair of Flight, Barr & Barr Worcester small vases, illustrated on the upturned example a typical version of th written mark, also the impressed initial-mark, to the right. $3\frac{3}{4}$ inches high. *c.* 1820.

550 A charming Flight, Barr & Barr small cup and saucer, showing the superb finish to the Worcester wares of this period. Written name-mark. Cup $2\frac{1}{4}$ inches high. *c.* 1820–25.

551 A superb-quality Kerr & Binns-period blue-ground vase, enamelled in the Limoges-style by Thomas Bott. Printed shield mark incorporating the date 1857 and Thomas Bott's monogram. $12\frac{3}{4}$ inches high.

552 A superb Royal Worcester ewer and stand enamelled on a deep-blue ground by Thomas Bott with subjects relating to the Norman Conquest. This example was shown at the 1871 Exhibition. Ewer $11\frac{1}{2}$ inches high. *c.* 1869–70.

553 A turquoise-ground Royal
Worcester vase, the figure-
painting by Josiah Rushton.
Printed mark with date-letter
for 1870. 14¾ inches high.

554 A blue-ground Royal
Worcester vase of unusual
form, richly gilt and jewelled.
Printed mark with date-
numerals for 1869. 15 inches
high.

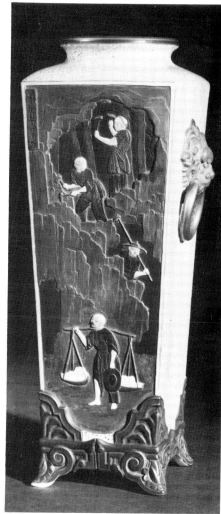

555 A Royal Worcester bottle-shaped vase of characteristic shape, very finely gilt in the Japanese style. The subject is one of the potting series. Printed mark. This example was shown at the 1872 Exhibition. 10¼ inches high.

556 A Royal Worcester vase in the popular Japanese style of the 1870s. Good use was made of matt golds of varying tints. Printed mark with year-letter for 1872. 11¼ inches high.

557 A richly gilt and ornately modelled Royal Worcester ewer, modelled by James Hadley in the popular Italian style. Printed mark with year-letter for 1885. 15½ inches high.

558 A superbly painted Royal Worcester dish or wall-plaque painted in 1881, one of the earliest essays in this now traditional style of Worcester decoration (see also Plate 566). Diameter 15¾ inches.

559 A typically attractive pair of Royal Worcester figures modelled by James Hadley in the Kate Greenaway style. These models were registered i 1882 and were continued for many years. Printed mark. 8½ inches high.

560 An attractive Royal Worcester table ornament modelled by James Hadley in his typical and popular Kate Greenaway manner. A good range of figures and groups was made in this style—these often incorporated baskets for sweets, nuts, etc. Matching candlesticks, condiments, centrepieces, etc., were also produced. Printed mark with year-letter for 1883. 8¼ inches high.

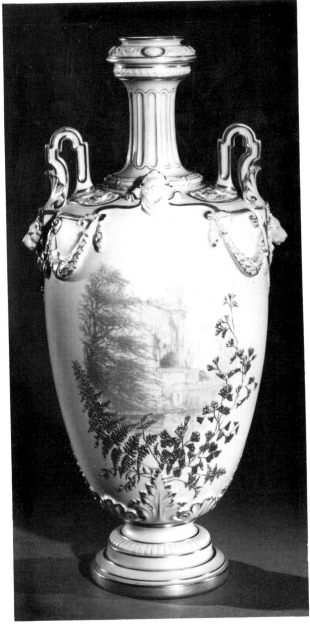

561 An ornately modelled
Royal Worcester vase of shape
1405, registered in 1890,
illustrating the soft, muted
colouring of the period.
Printed mark with year-dots
for 1894. 14¾ inches high.

562 An attractive Royal
Worcester vase of shape 1399,
registered in 1889. Printed
mark with year-letter for 1890.
14¼ inches high.

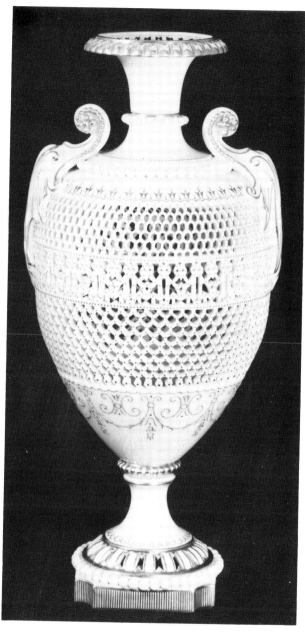

563 A fine and typical Royal
Worcester vase, the openwork
design being hand-cut by
George Owen, who specialised
in this type of reticulated work.
Shape-number 1969. Gold
printed mark with year-dots for
1909. Incised signature 'G.
Owen'. 8¾ inches high.

564 A graceful Royal Worcester
covered vase, the sheep and
landscape design signed and
painted by Harry Davis, one of
the celebrated Worcester artists
who specialised in misty
landscapes, Highland cattle,
etc. The dull, matt gilding is
typical of the 1900 period.
Printed mark with year-dots
for 1911. 15 inches high.

PRICES.

Ornament No.			£	s.	d.
Ornament No. 1	(G695)	Cattle	1	1	0
2	(H248⁰)	Pheasants	3	3	0
3	(2366)	Festoon Roses	2	14	0
4	(2336)	Cattle	4	6	3
5	(H211ᴬ)	Violets		13	6
6	(H158)	Violets		6	0
7	(1828)	Green Silk Drapery	3	7	6
8	(1827)	Red Silk Drapery	3	7	6
9	(1944)	Green Ground	1	13	9
10	(2330)	Sheep	5	1	3
11	(H271ᵇ)	Peacocks	1	5	6
12	(H179ᴬ)	Peacocks	2	12	6
13	(2210)	Poppies, &c.	2	16	3

Height from 3¾ inches (No. 6) to 14 inches (No. 10).

565 A page from a Royal Worcester catalogue of the 1910–12 period, showing typical shapes and styles of decoration—Highland cattle, peacocks, roses, etc. Sizes 3¾ to 14 inches.

566 A fine-quality Royal Worcester powder-blue-ground dessert service, the traditional fruit-panels painted by R. Sebright. This style of decoration dates from the 1880s (see Plate 558) and is still produced today. Printed mark with year-markings for 1923.

567 A pair of the celebrated Royal Worcester American birds, modelled by the late Miss Dorothy Doughty and issued in limited editions. A fine selection of these magnificent and technically superb pieces can be seen at the Worcester Works Museum. *c.* 1955–60.

Bibliography

MARK BOOKS

Chaffers, W. *Marks and Monograms on Pottery and Porcelain*, British section of latest 15th edition revised by G. A. Godden (William Reeves, 1965).

Cushion, J. P., *Pocket Book of British Ceramic Marks* (Faber, 1959; 4th revised edition, 1980).

Cushion, J. P., and W. B. Honey, *Handbook of Pottery and Porcelain Marks* (Faber, 1956; revised edition, 1980).

Godden, G. A., *Encyclopaedia of British Pottery and Porcelain Marks* (Barrie & Jenkins, 1964).

Godden, G. A., *Handbook of British Pottery and Porcelain Marks* (Barrie & Jenkins, revised edition 1983).

GENERAL STANDARD REFERENCE BOOKS

Atterbury, P. (ed.), *The History of Porcelain* (Orbis, 1982).

Berthoud, M., *An Anthology of British Cups* (Micawber, 1982).

An Anthology of British Teapots (Micawber, 1985).

Bradshaw, P., *Eighteenth Century English Porcelain Figures 1745–1795* (Antique Collectors' Club, 1981).

Bryant, G. E., *Chelsea Porcelain Toys* (Medici Society, 1925).

Burton, W., *A History and Description of English Porcelain* (Cassell, 1902).

Charleston, R. J. (ed.), *English Porcelain 1745–1850* (E. Benn, 1965).

Cushion, J. P., *Pottery and Porcelain Tablewares* (Studio Vista, 1977).

Eccles, H. and B. Rackham, *Analysed Specimens of English Porcelain* (Victoria and Albert Museum, 1922).

Fisher, S. W., *English Ceramics* (Ward Lock, 1966).

Godden, G. A., *Antique China and Glass under £5* (Arthur Barker, 1966).

British Porcelain, an Illustrated Guide (Barrie & Jenkins, 1974).

British Pottery, an Illustrated Guide (Barrie & Jenkins, 1974).

British Pottery & Porcelain 1780–1850 (Arthur Barker, 1963).

Godden's Guide to English Porcelain (Granada, 1978).

English China (Barrie & Jenkins, 1985).

Eighteenth-Century English Porcelain (Granada, 1985).

An Illustrated Encyclopaedia of British Pottery and Porcelain (Barrie & Jenkins, 1966).

Victorian Porcelain (Herbert Jenkins, 1961).

Godden, G. A., *The Encyclopaedia of British Porcelain Manufacturers* (Barrie & Jenkins, 1989).

Godden, G. A. (ed.), *Staffordshire Porcelain* (Granada, 1983).

Haggar, R. G., and W. Mankowitz, *The Concise Encyclopaedia of English Pottery and Porcelain* (A. Deutsch, 1957).

Honey, W. B., *English Pottery and Porcelain* (A. & C. Black, 1933; 5th edition, 1962).

Old English Porcelain (Faber, 1948; revised edition 1977).

Hughes, B. and T., *English Porcelain and Bone China 1743–1850* (Lutterworth Press, 1955).

Jewitt, L., *The Ceramic Art of Great Britain* (Virtue & Co., 1878; revised edition, 1883). A revised and re-illustrated edition covering only the period from 1800 onwards was published by Barrie & Jenkins in 1972.

Lane, A., *English Porcelain Figures of the Eighteenth Century* (Faber, 1961).

Rees, D., and M. G. Cawley, *A Pictorial Encyclopaedia of Goss China* (The Ceramic Book Company, Newport, Gwent, 1970).

Sandon, H., *British Pottery and Porcelain for Pleasure and Investment* (J. Gifford, 1969).

Savage, G. and H. Newman, *An Illustrated Dictionary of Ceramics* (Thames & Hudson, 1974).

Wills, G., *English Pottery and Porcelain* (Guinness Signatures, 1968).

SPECIALIST BOOKS ON INDIVIDUAL FACTORIES OR TYPES

S. Alcock

Godden, G. A. (ed.), *Staffordshire Porcelain*, Chapter 21 by Dr and Mrs G. Barnes (Granada, 1983).

Blue and White (porcelains)

Blue and White, Eighteenth Century English Soft Paste Porcelain, A. Amor exhibition catalogue, 1979.

Branyan, Lawrence, Neal French and John Sandon, *Worcester Blue and White Porcelain, 1751–1790* (Barrie & Jenkins, 1989).

Fisher, S. W., *English Blue and White Porcelain of the Eighteenth Century* (Batsford, 1947).

Godden, G. A., *An Introduction to English Blue and White Porcelains* (Geoffery Godden, China-man, Worthing, 1974).

Watney, B., *English Blue and White Porcelain of the Eighteenth Century* (Faber, 1963; revised edition, 1973).

C. Bourne

Godden, G. A. (ed.), *Staffordshire Porcelain*, Chapter 16 by G. A. Godden (Granada, 1983).

Bow

Adams, E. and D. Redstone, *Bow Porcelain* (Faber, 1981).

Bow Porcelain 1747–1775, A. Amor exhibition catalogue, 1982.

Gabszewicz, A., and G. Freeman, *Bow Porcelain* (Freeman Collection) (Lund Humphries, 1982).

Tait, H., *British Museum Catalogue of the 1959 Bow Exhibition.*

Bristol

Mackenna, F. Severne, *Champions Bristol Porcelain* (F. Lewis, Leigh-on-Sea, 1947).

Plymouth and Bristol Porcelain (Peter Stephens

Collection), A. Amor exhibition catalogue, 1978.

Caughley

Caughley Porcelains – a Bi-Centenary Exhibition, exhibition catalogue by M. Messenger (Shrewsbury Art Gallery, 1972).

Godden, G. A., *Caughley and Worcester Porcelains 1775–1800* (Herbert Jenkins, 1969; new edition, Antique Collectors' Club, 1981).

Chelsea

Adams, E., *Chelsea Porcelain* (Barrie & Jenkins, 1987).

Mackenna, F. Severne, *Chelsea Porcelain, the Gold Anchor Period* (F. Lewis, Leigh-on-Sea, 1952). *Chelsea Porcelain, the Red Anchor Wares* (F. Lewis, Leigh-on-Sea, 1951). *Chelsea Porcelain, the Triangle and Raised Anchor Wares* (F. Lewis, Leigh-on-Sea, 1948).

Coalport

Godden, G. A., *Coalport and Coalbrookdale Porcelains* (Herbert Jenkins, 1970; new edition, Antique Collectors' Club, 1981).

Daniel

Berthoud, M., *The Daniel Tableware Patterns* (Micawber, 1982). *H. & R. Daniel 1822–1846* (Micawber, 1980).

Godden, G. A. (ed.), *Staffordshire Porcelains*, Chapter 19 by G. A. Godden (Granada, 1983).

Davenport

Davenport Pottery and Porcelain, Blackburn Museum exhibition catalogue, 1978.

Godden, G. A. (ed.), *Staffordshire Porcelain*, Chapter 10 by T. A. Lockett (Granada, 1983).

Godden, G. & Lockett, T., *Davenport, Earthenware & Glass 1794–1887* (Barrie & Jenkins, 1989).

Lockett, T. A., *Davenport Pottery and Porcelain 1794–1887* (David & Charles, 1972).

Derby

Barrett, F. A., and A. L. Thorpe, *Derby Porcelain* (Faber, 1971).

Bradley, H. G., *Ceramics of Derbyshire 1750–1978* (privately published, 1978).

Gilhespy, F. B., *Crown Derby Porcelain* (F. Lewis, Leigh-on-Sea, 1951). *Derby Porcelain* (Spring Books, 1961).

Haslem, J., *The Old Derby China Factory* (G. Bell & Sons, 1876).

Twitchett, J., *Derby Porcelain* (Barrie & Jenkins, 1980).

Twitchett, J., and B. Bailey, *Royal Crown Derby* (Barrie & Jenkins, 1976).

Hicks & Meigh

Godden, G. A. (ed.), *Staffordshire Porcelain*, Chapter 17 by G. A. Godden (Granada, 1983).

Hilditch (Hilditch & Hopwood)

Godden, G. A. (ed.), *Staffordshire Porcelain*, Chapter 18 by P. Helm (Granada, 1983).

Liverpool

Hills, M., *The Liverpool Porcelains* Northern Ceramic Society, 1985).

Smith, A., *The Illustrated Guide to Liverpool Herculaneum Pottery* (Barrie & Jenkins, 1970).

Watney, B., *English Blue and White Porcelain of the Eighteenth Century* (Faber, 1963; revised edition, 1973).

Longton Hall

Godden, G. A. (ed.), *Staffordshire Porcelain*, Chapter 2 by A. R. Mountford (Granada, 1983).

Watney, B., *Longton Hall Porcelain* (Faber, 1957).

Lowestoft

Godden, G. A., *The Illustrated Guide to Lowestoft Porcelain* (Herbert Jenkins, 1969).

Lowestoft Porcelains (Antique Collectors' Club, 1985).

Smith, S., *Lowestoft Porcelain in Norwich Castle Museum*, vols I & II (Norwich Museum Service, 1975).

Spencer, C., *Early Lowestoft* (Ainsworth & Nelson, 1981).

Machin

Godden, G. A. (ed.), *Staffordshire Porcelain*, Chapter 13 by P. Miller (Granada, 1983).

Mason

Godden, G. A., *Godden's Guide to Mason's China and the Ironstone Wares* (Antique Collectors' Club, 1980).

The Illustrated Guide to Mason's Patent Ironstone China (Barrie & Jenkins, 1971).

Godden, G. A. (ed.), *Staffordshire Porcelain*, Chapter 11 by R. G. Haggar (Granada, 1983).

Haggar, R. G., *The Masons of Lane Delph* (Lund Humphries, 1952).

Haggar, R. G., and E. Adams, *Mason Porcelain and Ironstone 1796–1853* (Faber, 1977).

Minton

Godden, G. A., *Minton Pottery and Porcelain of the First Period 1793–1850* (Herbert Jenkins, 1968).

Victorian Porcelain (Herbert Jenkins, 1961).

Godden, G. A. (ed.), *Staffordshire Porcelain*, Chapter 9 by G. A. Godden (Granada, 1983).

Nantgarw

John, W. D., *Nantgarw Porcelain* (Ceramic Book Co., Newport, Gwent, 1948; supplement, 1956).

Nance, E. M., *The Pottery and Porcelain of Swansea and Nantgarw* (Batsford, 1942).

Neale & Co. (Neale & Wilson)

Godden, G. A. (ed.), *Staffordshire Porcelain*, Chapter 4 by G. A. Godden (Granada, 1983).

New Hall

Godden, G. A. (ed.), *Staffordshire Porcelain*, Chapter 5 by D. Holgate (Granada, 1983).

Holgate, D., *New Hall* (Faber, 1987).

de Saye Hutton, A., *A Guide to New Hall Porcelain Patterns* (Barrie & Jenkins, 1990).

Stringer, G. E., *New Hall Porcelain* (Art Trade Press, 1949).

Parian

Godden, G. A., *Victorian Porcelain* (Herbert Jenkins, 1961).

Shinn, C. and D., *The Illustrated Guide to Victorian Parian China* (Barrie & Jenkins, 1971).

Pinxton

Exley, C. L., *The Pinxton China Factory* (Mr & Mrs Coke-Steel, Sutton-on-the-Hill, 1963).

Plymouth

Mackenna, F. S., *Cookworthy's Plymouth and Bristol Porcelain* (F. Lewis, Leigh-on-Sea, 1947).

Plymouth and Bristol Porcelain (Peter Stephens Collection), A. Amor exhibition catalogue, 1978.

Watney, B., *English Blue and White Porcelain of the Eighteenth Century* (Faber, 1963; revised edition, 1973).

Ridgway

Godden, G. A., *The Illustrated Guide to Ridgway Porcelains* (Barrie & Jenkins, 1972).
Ridgway Porcelains (Antique Collectors' Club, 1985).
Godden, G. A. (ed.), *Staffordshire Porcelain*, Chapter 12 by G. A. Godden (Granada, 1983).

Rockingham

Cox, Alwyn and Angela, *Rockingham Pottery and Porcelain 1745–1842* (Faber, 1983).
Eaglestone, A. A., and T. A. Lockett, *The Rockingham Pottery* (Rotherham Library and Museum, 1964; revised edition, David & Charles, 1973).
Rice, D. G., *The Illustrated Guide to Rockingham Porcelain* (Barrie & Jenkins, 1971).
Ornamental Rockingham Porcelains (Adam Publishing Co., 1965).

Spode

Godden, G. A. (ed.), *Staffordshire Porcelain*, Chapter 8 by Robert Copeland (Granada, 1983).
Hayden, A., *Spode and his Successors* (Cassell & Co., 1924).
Whiter, L., *Spode: A History of the Family, Factory and Wares from 1733 to 1833* (Barrie & Jenkins, revised 1987 edition).

Swansea

John, W. D., *Swansea Porcelain* (Ceramic Book Co., Newport, Gwent, 1957).
Jones, E. A. & Joseph, Sir L., *Swansea Porcelains, Shapes and Decoration* (D. Brown & Sons Ltd, 1988).
Nance, E. M., *The Pottery and Porcelain of Swansea and Nantgarw* (Batsford, 1942).

Turner

Godden, G. A. (ed.), *Staffordshire Porcelain*, Chapter 6 by D. Holgate and G. A. Godden (Granada, 1983).

Wedgwood (Porcelain only)

Godden, G. A. (ed.), *Staffordshire Porcelain*, Chapter 14 by J. K. des Fontaines (Granada, 1983).
See also page 406.

Worcester

Barrett, F. A., *Worcester Porcelain* (Faber, 1963; revised edition, 1966).
Binns, R. W., *A Century of Potting in the City of Worcester* (B. Quaritch, 1865; 2nd edition, 1877).
Worcester China 1852–1897 (B. Quaritch, 1897).
Branyan, L., N. French and J. Sandon, *Worcester Blue and White Porcelain 1751–1790* (Barrie & Jenkins, 1989).
Godden, G. A., *Chamberlain–Worcester Porcelain 1788–1852* (Barrie & Jenkins, 1982).
Marshall, H. Rissik, *Coloured Worcester Porcelain of the First Period* (Ceramic Book Co., Newport, Gwent, 1954).
Sandon, H., *Flight and Barr Worcester Porcelains 1783–1840* (Antique Collectors' Club, 1978).
The Illustrated Guide to Worcester Porcelain 1751–1793 (Herbert Jenkins, 1969).
Royal Worcester Porcelain (Barrie & Jenkins, 1973; third edition 1978).
The Sandon Guide to Royal Worcester Figures 1900–1970 Alderman Press, 1987).

COLLECTORS' MAGAZINES

Antique Collecting, Antique Collectors' Club, 5 Church Street, Woodbridge, Suffolk, IP12 1DS.
Antique Collector, National Magazine House, 72 Broadwick Street, London W1V 2BP.
Apollo, Apollo Magazines Ltd, 22 Davies Street, London W1Y 1LH.
Collectors Guide (incorporating, from 1982, *Art and Antiques*), IPC Magazines Ltd, King's Reach Tower, Stamford Street, London SE1 9LS.

Index